You, the Leader

Women *at* Work

Inspiring conversations, advancing together.

The **HBR WOMEN AT WORK SERIES** spotlights the real challenges and opportunities women experience throughout their careers. With interviews from the popular podcast of the same name and related articles, stories, and research, these books provide inspiration and advice for taking on issues at work such as inequity, advancement, and building community. Featuring detailed discussion guides, this series will help you spark important conversations about where we're at and how to move forward.

Books in the series include:

Making Real Connections

Speak Up, Speak Out

You, the Leader

Women *at* Work

Inspiring conversations, advancing together.

You, the Leader

Harvard Business Review Press
Boston, Massachusetts

Printed in the United States of America

10 9 8 7 6 5 4 3 2 1

Cataloging-in-Publication data is forthcoming.

ISBN: 978-1-64782-225-5

eISBN: 978-1-64782-226-2

The paper used in this publication meets the requirements of the American National Standard for Permanence of Paper for Publications and Documents in Libraries and Archives Z39.48-1992.

CONTENTS

INTRODUCTION

Becoming a Leader

by Amy Bernstein, cohost of *Women at Work*

Maybe some people are born leaders. I certainly wasn't one of them—a lesson I learned painfully a few years back when a work pal took me to task.

We'd just had a meeting, and I, as usual, had said absolutely nothing. The reason for my reticence was fear of ridicule. Meetings at my (mostly male) organization were like blood sport: Editors would shoot down each other's ideas mercilessly (this was long before I came to HBR). I certainly wasn't going to lay myself open to their barbs. And yet I knew I needed to raise my profile if I wanted to get ahead. I felt thwarted and miserable.

My friend knew all that when she marched into my office, shut the door, and let me have it: "You know a lot about that topic, and you should have been leading the conversation. Why were you so quiet? What are you waiting for—someone to give you permission to lead? Because that's not going to happen."

That was the gut punch I needed. She was right: I had to take responsibility for my stalled career, figure out how to deal with the reality of my workplace, and show up as a leader. But how?

It turns out that many women grapple with these same questions. In the years we've been producing *Women at Work*, the HBR podcast I cohost with Amy Gallo and Emily Caulfield (and, in the past, with Sarah Green Carmichael and Nicole Torres), listeners have shared their own stories of stagnation and frustration. They tell us how they struggle to be heard, get their proper credit, and be treated with respect. They ask for advice on dealing with the barriers women face at work, from unsupportive bosses to unfair policies. They want our help as they strive to emerge as leaders themselves. Our listeners are coping with the same biases and self-doubt that we hosts do, even at our different career stages. On *Women at Work*, we are just trying to help each other get where we want to go.

I wish this podcast had been around back when I was going through the agonizing growth process. Understanding that I wasn't seen as a leader was painful. It wasn't just that I didn't grasp what leadership is—a way of moving through the world with vision, determination, and empathy. It was that I didn't *see* myself as a leader, as the kind of person who can motivate and inspire others.

So much of leadership is about visualizing ourselves in the role—and ensuring others do, too. That takes self-knowledge and conviction. As leadership consultant Muriel Maignan Wilkins has noted on the podcast (and says in chapter 5), we must confront the myth that "leadership looks one way, which is, quite frankly, the white masculine way." There is no one right way to be a leader. You have to figure out who you are and what you stand for. But you also need to know that you *want* to lead. You have to "own it," says Wilkins.

One of the biggest challenges to seeing ourselves (and having others see us) as leaders is the gap between who we believe we are and how the world expects us to behave. In chapter 4, Tasha Eurich, an organizational psychologist, observes that while "the average woman isn't underestimating herself as a leader, she has a slightly more nuanced challenge: She may not be confident that others value her contributions." That's a big one for me. Having sat through too many meetings where I was repeatedly interrupted and where my contributions were ignored until a man repeated them, it was easy for me to believe that my colleagues didn't respect me. But once you understand that this kind of behavior is disgracefully common, you learn that it's really not about you or your ideas. And it becomes easier to call people out on their bad behavior. On this point, Eurich's advice—"To overcome the tendency to rely too heavily on others' views, women can develop their own picture of who they are"—is pure gold.

Understanding that women start out at a disadvantage is vital to addressing it. We know that women don't get the same treatment as men in the workplace: There's ample evidence that they're paid less, have fewer opportunities to develop and advance, are unfairly assessed in performance evaluations, and receive less actionable feedback. The list goes on. Many of the barriers lie in policy and process; bias is baked into the system and reinforced by unquestioning behavior and tradition.

Other forces are subtler and perhaps more confounding because they're harder to pinpoint and address. Consider the double bind—the contradiction between what society expects of us as women on the one hand and leaders on the other. As women, we're expected to be warm and nice, but as leaders we're supposed to prove we're tough and competent. We're supposed to be caring yet demanding, collaborative yet authoritative, approachable yet distant, passionate yet unemotional. I admit I struggled with the constant balancing act. How could I be seen as an assertive, self-confident leader—one whose views matter—without coming off as domineering and unlikable?

This book looks at all of these issues and offers solutions for women—and those around them—to overcome them. Think of it as a crash course in leadership for women. It collects valuable tips, advice, and discussion in four key areas: finding your authentic self, showing your leadership potential, advocating for yourself, and supporting the women around you (even if you're not a woman). It aims to help aspiring female leaders better understand what it means to live into leadership authentically, ensure that others see their potential, and speak up with confidence, all while navigating the biases and gendered assumptions around them.

Even now, years after that excruciating conversation about my leadership—or lack thereof—I am grateful to that coworker who scolded me after that meeting. She jolted me into consciousness about my own values and commitment to myself. It was brutal at the time, but it forced me to figure out who I am and who I want to be. And that is the first step to becoming a leader.

SECTION ONE

Find Your Authentic Self

1

Lead with Authenticity

A conversation with Tina Opie

Authenticity is what it feels like when you can bring your whole self to work—when your behavior matches your intentions. But there's a challenge for women who want to be authentic at work. We're daughters, mothers, sisters, and bosses, and all these different roles can be tough to reconcile. So while authentic leadership is often viewed as geared toward a single norm, as women we live in a multipolar world. How can we be true to ourselves when there are so many competing selves?

Tina Opie is an associate professor at Babson College. She sat down with *Women at Work* cohosts Amy Bernstein, Sarah Green Carmichael, and Nicole Torres to talk about what feels authentic to us and what doesn't, particularly when it comes to emotions at work.

SARAH GREEN CARMICHAEL: I worked with a woman once whose boss told her, "You have a lot of potential—I can see you moving into management. But if you want to do that, you need to dress differently and you should start wearing makeup." Everyone in this case was a woman, but my peer was furious. Is it sexist to give someone that kind of advice?

TINA OPIE: We have to differentiate between how we want the world to be and how the world actually is. Would I like that advice to never be heard or uttered? Would I like it if the way you want to go to work was completely fine as long as you're doing an amazing job? That's the kind of world I want to live in, and the kind of world that I've dedicated my research and teaching toward building. But unfortunately, that is not the world in which we live.

We live in a world where impressions matter, and where appearance is highly connected to impressions. The way that humans categorize other people is instantaneous. And because of those types of connections, we automatically think, "*This* kind of person is going to be more professional. *This* kind of person is not going to be." If you happen to fall into the latter category, you may have some additional work to do to demonstrate that you are, in fact, fierce, professional, or amazing. But that may come after that initial impression.

NICOLE TORRES: Aside from appearance, how else do we think about authenticity in the workplace?

TINA: Well, it could be the way that you communicate. I was once told that I was too ethnic because I speak with my hands. But the clients loved me. They said, "You're such a great storyteller." So the way that you communicate, your accent, or the way that you articulate anger, disagreement, and conflict all matter for authenticity. Some people will avoid anger at all costs; others will dive right in. For me, it is authentic to convey anger, but that's considered unprofessional in some settings.

Imagine a setting where you're direct with your supervisor, subordinate, or colleague and say, "Listen, that was my idea in the meeting. We talked about it. Explain to me why you took credit for it."

NICOLE: I could never imagine saying that.

TINA: But ask yourself why. Some of it is about personality, but in many professional contexts you're going to be considered bad if you advocate for yourself, especially if you do that in front of the group.

SARAH: When we talk about leaders being authentic, a lot of what we talk about is that we want to invite in happy feelings to the workplace. We say we want people to bring their whole selves to work, but we really mean those parts of themselves that are shiny and happy. We don't usually mean anger, especially for women.

TINA: You're absolutely right. Women experience significant backlash when they express anger in the workplace—Tori Brescoll at the Yale School of Management has done some work on that. But then Ashleigh Shelby Rosette at Duke's Fuqua School of Business, Robert Livingston at the Harvard Kennedy School, and some other folks have done some additional research that shows that this may have to do with intersectionality, because Black women don't receive as much backlash as white women do when expressing anger in the workforce.

I have never understood the visceral negative reaction to anger in the workplace. Now, I'm not talking about someone going up and down the aisles and yelling at people, cursing people out, physical violence, or throwing things around. Anger means displeasure, annoyance. It's a signal that something is awry or unjust. Why is it bad to express that?

Of course, we have to think about the way that we channel that emotion and the way that we communicate those ideas at work. Women in particular have to be mindful of that. Women who can figure out how to use their anger in a productive way may find themselves at an advantage.

Have you all been angry in the workplace? What have you done? Have you gone to your cube or office? Have you called a friend? Gone into the bathroom and cried? I'd be curious to know if you all have seen examples of when anger has been successfully used.

AMY BERNSTEIN: You just made me think about the instances when I've been angry and when I've cried. There are two kinds of anger as I've experienced them. One is the hurt anger: *I can't believe you just did that to me.* That is really difficult for me. I always question whether or not this is justified and how much of it is my fault. I go through that checklist of reasons not to deal with it, and when I have dealt with it, it's brought change that I needed.

But there's another kind of anger that I have had more frequently, which is when things aren't done the way I've asked for them to be done. I run a team and an operation; if I believe that my requests have been countermanded, I get angry and I will say so. I'll call people out for it, but I'll do it privately, usually. If it is impeding progress for the organization, that will make me quite angry, and I can be articulate about it. The other one, holy cow, I just go up in flames.

TINA: What's interesting is that when it's about you in that way, we give ourselves permission to be mad: *This is about the work, so I have permission to be angry because if I don't say something, the organization suffers.* Here we are as women who want to save the organization. So we're willing to go to bat for that kind of anger.

I would also say that we as women may be more willing to articulate our anger if someone has been unjust to someone *else* or we see someone treating one of our subordinates unfairly—Here I am, angry woman, hands on hips, head to the side, *what are you doing?* But if they had done the same thing to us, we don't give ourselves permission to articulate that anger and to address the injustices that are personal.

SARAH: I've spent most of my career in HBR, and my experience of our company culture is that visible displays of anger are not welcome. On the whole, this anti-anger culture works for me because I'm a conflict-avoidant person. That said, there have been times when I have felt angry at work. The older I have gotten, the more I have been willing to call it anger and the more I've been able to decide what to do with it as opposed to just feeling it.

NICOLE: It seems related to women being expected not to show too much emotion at work. Even being passionate about something can be misinterpreted as being too emotional. That line gets put on women much more often than on men.

AMY: I also think it's connected to our fear of directness. I get called out on that occasionally. In a polite culture, like ours, being direct can be misinterpreted as being angry or rude when all you're trying to do is be clear, because a lack of clarity in my view leads to all kinds of problems. Plus, I'm a New Yorker; it's in my DNA. Tina, what are your thoughts?

TINA: I absolutely agree. You're still getting at the idea that there are organizational cultural notions of what is and isn't professional. How you express yourself in the workplace is connected to authenticity.

I come from a very direct family. We're from the South, and people often think about Southern gentility. But we're a Black Southern family, and let me tell you—if somebody comes to the house and they're rude, we might not say it in front of them, but we will talk about it for days. The interesting thing is that as I grew older, I was known as the one who was direct, who was forthright, so my mother would say, "Go get 'em, Tina. Go tell 'em what the deal is." Because that was my personality.

I absolutely think as a woman in the workplace, I have been slapped on the wrist for being too direct. But I've also tried to figure out how to work around that. I will say to someone when they come to me and ask a question, "Do you want to hear the truth? Do you want to hear what I really think? Or do you want me to just say something to appease the situation?" If you tell me you really want to hear what I think, I'm going to be direct. People know that about me, and for some reason people like that. I actually think we could adjust our cultures and workplaces so that being direct with kindness would be valued, as opposed to being indirect, which doesn't necessarily have a kind intention behind it. Someone may not want to hurt your feelings, but they also may not want to give you the direct critical feedback that would help you evolve into a better employee.

SARAH: My background is a white Anglo-Saxon Protestant New Englander, and my family is not direct. In the workplace, I have always struggled with how I can be indirect but clear and nice, versus what feels to me like being direct and clear but mean. Nicole, what about you?

NICOLE: Background? Very indirect. We're suppressors of emotion. We seethe if we're sad or angry. It was not a very emotional household, and I am not a very emotional person. When I come into work, I don't consider myself very indirect, but I think I'm very polite in my emails, though asking for things can be kind of a challenge: *This will be a great idea; this is great for both of us—*

SARAH: You may be the most polite person in our office.

NICOLE: I'm very polite. I love exclamation points! I want people to feel my positive energy going to them. I think that's internalized from growing up and not really getting to be angry or getting to show anger or even ask for things directly.

TINA: I'm putting you on the spot, Nicole. Do you identify as Asian?

NICOLE: Uh-huh.

TINA: From what country?

NICOLE: Philippines.

TINA: I asked because there are stereotypes. In the workplace, Asian people are known as model minorities. Really polite, they will get the work done and focus on the task, but they're not leaders. Have you heard that stereotype before?

NICOLE: Oh, yeah. We've published research on that.

TINA: I've read that research and actually have counseled some of my students of Asian descent because that's something that they encounter. My question is, when you said you're not very emotional, is it that you don't feel the emotions? Or that you don't want to express the emotion?

NICOLE: I feel these emotions. Not knowing how to express them or what's appropriate to express is probably a big question that I think about subconsciously. I think it is cultural, and that norms of my household growing up and the trajectory that was laid out for me is very different than the expectations and path that I envision for myself now. Trying to advance in the workplace, trying to lead and be heard—that's very different than the role I was expected to play growing up: *Do really well in school, don't talk back, get good grades, get a good job, don't cause a fuss.*

TINA: We all have our cultural upbringing. We go into a workplace context and have to figure out where we as authentic individuals reside and how we navigate those spaces. Because if you want to express your emotion but you feel like you don't know how to, that's one thing. But if you feel like you have to express emotion because the workplace is forcing you to do that, then that's still inauthentic.

AMY: Herminia Ibarra of London Business School wrote this great HBR article, "The Authenticity Paradox." One of the points she made that really resonated for me was that when you think about authenticity, particularly someone who's closer to the beginning of her career, you have to try on different personas to see which one feels comfortable. Because the person who graduated from college a few years ago probably isn't going to be the one who thrives in any workplace, right? You learn, you grow, you bump into a few things, you find the right way forward for yourself. Does that resonate for you, Nicole?

NICOLE: Yeah. She said in that piece that you don't want to have too rigid a definition of authenticity. What I would love to know is what's the difference between being inauthentic and then just being pushed out of your comfort zone. With the latter you do need to evolve in the workplace and as a leader.

TINA: For me, authenticity is about being your best self. There's some research that has said: *Keep your authentic self at home. Nobody wants to see your authentic self—it's nasty.* Well, that's not the authentic self that I'm talking about. It's one thing to be driving, see someone do something that makes you angry, and give them the finger. Some people would say that's being authentic. But I would say it's not. That is being under stress or duress. If I had time to stop and reflect and didn't allow my emotions to carry me away, I wouldn't do that. Because that's not what I value; that doesn't align with the values that I authentically hold.

SARAH: A work example is how women can adjust their communication style to be heard more in meetings. Rather than phrasing something as a question, such as, "How about we do this?" instead saying, "My strong recommendation is this." Does it feel inauthentic when you are consciously trying to change the way that you talk to be heard?

TINA: It's difficult to know because some of that may come from career counseling and career advice that will help women, men—everyone. But some of it is subtle cues to conform; to speak louder; to use more declarative statements; to be more emphatic; to stand up, spread yourself out, and possess the room; to get in there and command the space. Are we talking about a football field or a conference room? What if you have someone who has a softer voice, who is brilliant but can argue and present both sides? Don't we have room at the table or in the workplace for that kind of voice as well?

I think we can quickly go down a road where we're advising women in ways like, "Speak in a deeper voice." Is that really necessary? If they're communicating the ideas, do they need to communicate in a particular way?

AMY: How is that different from how you dress?

TINA: That's the question. I don't know. Because we're trying to figure out the boundary lines, right? We're trying to figure out how this person can be authentic and excel in the workplace.

I do not have much of a Southern accent unless I'm angry or really tired. And that is because my parents raised us to not have a Southern accent, because they recognized that it might be inhibiting to our academic and career success. Would I be more authentic if I still had my Southern accent? I don't know. I was willing to give that up. I'm not willing to relax my hair though. That's the line for me.

SARAH: Do you think that it is possible for a woman to be a truly authentic leader?

TINA: I do think it's possible for a woman to be an authentic leader—a person who is expressing themselves, who is reflected in the values that they want to bring to the workplace, who is willing to share the pros and cons with the people who are following them.

What I'm struggling with is *authentic leadership*. The definition of it can shift depending on what you're talking about. Do we mean someone who's honest and transparent? Or do we mean someone who is pursuing their best self, who is working to take the perspectives of the people who follow them so that they can take that into consideration when they're making decisions? I think it's possible for women to be authentic and to be leaders in that way.

I do not think it's necessarily limited to certain kinds of women, but I do think it's harder for women. The less power you have, the more challenging it can be to be authentic, period. If you're an hourly worker who is dependent upon your employer and they tell you to wear an apron and straighten your hair, you may be more inclined to do that than if you are the CEO of an organization. We have to be sensitive to the fact that it's not as easy for everyone, and power rears its head and impacts women's and men's ability to be authentic in the workplace and to be authentic leaders.

Adapted from "Lead with Authenticity," Women at Work *podcast season 1, episode 3, February 9, 2018.*

2

How Women Manage the Gendered Norms of Leadership

by Wei Zheng, Ronit Kark, and Alyson Meister

A wealth of research shows that female leaders, much more than their male counterparts, face the need to be warm and nice (what society traditionally expects from women) as well as competent and tough (what society traditionally expects from men and leaders).[1] The problem is that these qualities are often seen as opposites. This creates a catch-22 and double bind for women leaders. Carly Fiorina, the former CEO of Hewlett-Packard, depicted it this way in her book *Tough Choices*: "In the chat rooms around Silicon Valley, from the time I arrived until long after I left HP, I was routinely referred to as either a 'bimbo' or a 'bitch'—too soft or too hard, and presumptuous, besides."

To alleviate this double bind, societal expectations—for what it means to be a woman and what it takes to lead—must change. But until we get there, women still have to navigate these tensions. We wanted to know how successful women do it day-to-day, so we conducted extensive interviews with 64 senior women leaders (all at the VP level or higher) from 51 organizations in the United States: CEOs, general managers, and executives across functions, working in various industries.[2] We found that there are four paradoxes, all stemming from the need to be both tough and nice, that these women confront. We also identified five strategies they use to manage them.

Four Balancing Acts

Paradox 1: Being demanding yet caring

The female executives told us they must demand high performance from others while also demonstrating that they care about them. For example, Norma (all names have been changed to protect privacy), an HR executive in financial services, recalled how, in a past project, her perseverance led to successful project outcomes but also earned her some negative feedback: "I remember a program that I designed that everyone was doubting . . . and I truly just knew deep in my heart and . . . gut that it was going to work. So I kept pushing forward . . . and it was a huge, huge success. . . . I've gotten feedback on being intimidating and that kind of stuff. Would I get the same feedback if I were a man?"

Paradox 2: Being authoritative yet participative

This paradox is the trade-off between asserting one's competence and admitting one's vulnerability, including when asking others to collaborate. On the one hand, women leaders learned to project authoritativeness, because without doing so, they risked being perceived as not credible, especially at the beginning of a new business engagement. They learned to "toughen up," "speak louder," and "act decisively."

On the other hand, to prevent being perceived as arrogant, women leaders were also quick to acknowledge their own weaknesses and work with others. For example, Claire, a general manager in manufacturing, commented: "I'd learned about [my] tendencies of being directive. I'm having to manage and maybe take it down and go slower, go slow to go fast, to bring people along and to ensure that we have alignment."

Paradox 3: Advocating for oneself yet serving others

The third paradox involves meeting one's needs and goals as well as others'. Focusing too heavily on one side can cause serious trouble. For example, Cameron, a strategy executive in an accounting firm, told us how she would share her knowledge with others, only to later feel taken advantage of when they failed to reciprocate. By contrast, Meredith, a general manager in health services, was almost removed from a leadership team because she was seen as too aggressive in negotiating with internal stakeholders in order to promote her own goals.

Paradox 4: Maintaining distance yet being approachable

Our study subjects sometimes struggled to be seen as leaders, rather than just colleagues and team members, while also developing close relationships. To generate respect, women leaders kept a distance from others, maintaining an impersonal "leadership presence" that was marked as "professional," "objective," and "serious." At the same time, they noticed that doing so may create impressions of being "stiff," "egocentric," and "apathetic," making it difficult to earn trust and commitment.

To bridge this gap, many women explicitly and emphatically worked to convey the intimate human side of themselves, so they were instead seen as "accessible," "warm," "social," "personable," "friendly," "informal," and "easy to connect with." Dawn, CEO of a nonprofit organization, explained how she did this through something as simple as clothing: "I always try to dress just ever so slightly more formal than employees, except on Fridays when I dress very informal to show that I'm also not stiff and unapproachable. Generally we have fun, but . . . there is a little bit of distancing that I try to maintain. . . . I want people to see that I'm fair-minded and not playing favorites."

Strategies for Managing the Tensions

Our findings suggest that to successfully navigate these paradoxes, women first need to become aware of them, teasing out the different tensions rolled up into the central nice/tough double bind. Then, they can develop and customize a repertoire of strategies to manage them, thereby enhancing their effectiveness and resilience. We identified five:

Adapt to the situation

Most of our study subjects told us that they demonstrate niceness and toughness in different situations, toward different audiences. For example, to signal both distance and approachability, Melissa, a general manager in a manufacturing firm, said: "I specifically don't sit at the head of the table at certain times. [It] depends on the meeting and the environment. [Sometimes,] I want to send the signal I'm just one of the team today, and other times I want to be very clear that I'm here to make a decision, and then I take a slightly different stance."

Go in order

Another strategy is to be nice (or caring and collaborative) first, then tough (or demanding and directive). First, you build relationships, establish trust, and engage people, and then you follow up with harder behavior or language to challenge the status quo or achieve goals. For example, Marilyn, a general manager in a financial services firm, talked about her philosophy of working with others: "I think it's just [building] that day-to-day relationship where people want to help you succeed. And so when you . . . advocate for something, people generally bend over backwards to figure out how to help you get it done."

Similarly, Ruth, a product development executive in manufacturing, talked about an incident in which she pushed to shut down a project that some of her peers considered their "baby." She was able to do so without incurring resentment because she had first "invested a lot of time in developing strong collaborative relationships," which was later helpful, since then, she said, "You can get past some of the politics. . . . I'm not trying to make you look bad. I really do just want to work for the betterment of the business."

Look for win-wins

Many women we talked to focused on identifying opportunities where niceness and toughness converge—what they sometimes called a "win-win" strategy. For example, Dorothy, a general manager in health services, described her mindset this way: "The most important thing is understanding what are the values, the traits, the goals of that person that you're trying to influence. . . . So, I've always tried to know what it is that I'm trying to achieve, [and] tie that back to something that I know they want to achieve."

Be tough on tasks and soft on people

With this strategy, women leaders focused on simultaneously being nice to people and tough on tasks. For example, Sally, a state legislator, shared her experience: "I learned that we could vehemently disagree on an issue, and when we walked out of the room, we were friends. I really came to see the importance of being able to separate [that] out."

Denise, a strategy executive in a financial organization, shared another example: When a colleague presented an unsatisfactory proposal, she used a soft approach to deliver a hard message: "I wanted to lay enough on the table to say, 'Boy, this is very interesting. . . . Can we do some more research on this? Can we test this against some other organizations?' That's an example of where you can get an idea across without saying, 'Hey, listen, I think this is really dumb, and we're not going to do it.' I'm much more effective as a leader if I lead with a question."

Reframe

We found that the women we studied also tried to reframe what it meant to be nice and tough. They focused on connecting the two and reinforcing positive associations. This involved recasting behaviors that might be considered weaknesses as strengths. For example, they described displays of vulnerability as reflecting inner confidence—feeling secure enough to reveal their own faults and weaknesses. Shannon, a president in a manufacturing company, explained, "I am very confident in saying, 'I don't know the answer but I'm keen to find out' or 'I don't know the answer but I know I have the ability to find out.'"

Another approach was to frame assertive behaviors that others might find threatening as originating from genuine care. For example, several women described giving negative feedback or voicing disagreements as trying to help others.

In the long run, organizations and society must produce systematic change to alleviate conflicting expectations for women and additional hurdles for their leadership. But as long as women face the double bind, they will need to find ways to manage it.

Adapted from content posted on hbr.org, November 28, 2018 (product #H04NZT).

3

Make Room in Your Work Life for the Rest of Your Self

by Brianna Barker Caza, Lakshmi Ramarajan, Erin Reid, and Stephanie Creary

Shonda Rhimes, the television producer and creator of shows including *Grey's Anatomy* and *Scandal*, is an entertainment industry titan. In a TED talk, she described her deep passion for her work: "When I'm hard at work, when I'm deep in it, there is no other feeling. . . . It is hitting every high note. It is running a marathon. It is being Beyoncé. And it is all of those things at the same time. I love working. . . . A hum begins in my brain, and it grows and it grows and that hum sounds like the open road, and I could drive it forever."[1]

Yet, despite Rhimes's passion and success, her single-minded investment in her work drove her to the point of burnout and exhaustion. She had stopped enjoying her life. To heal, she refocused on the parts of herself—a mother, a friend, a sister, an athlete—that had been neglected because of her tunnel vision. She became more outspoken about being a woman, a mother, and an African American in the entertainment industry: "Work's hum is still a piece of me, it is just no longer all of me," she said.

Rhimes's story of overinvesting in a single facet of herself—her work identity—and then burning out is unfortunately all too common; and her story of recovering by reviving other identities is all too rare. If the hum of your career has become so deafening that you struggle to hear those other parts of your life, you're not alone. Crafting and sustaining a multifaceted identity is challenging for today's employees and their organizations. The greedy nature of our work (asking us to wear more hats, to do more, to always be on), combined with the demands of our personal lives and social pressure to be and focus on just one thing, means we need to learn how to manage our portfolio of identities and the expectations that come with them.[2]

Through interviews with hundreds of workers—consultants, managers, medical professionals, architects, entrepreneurs, authors, lawyers, knowledge workers, fitness professionals, educators, military officers, and journalists—we have found that the right strategies can help us harness our complex identities to benefit ourselves, our relationships, and our organizations. Our research suggests that making some simple changes to how you think about yourself, how you act out your identities, and how you make space for others' identities can help you successfully manage your multiple identities, and thrive as a complex and whole person.

Change How You Think About Yourself

First, you must take command of your own story. Doing so requires reflecting on your complexity, moving away from zero-sum thinking about who you are, and creating and leveraging connections between your identities.

Reflect on your complexity

How do you currently think about who you are and the things you are doing? Do you feel as though you are a jack-of-all-trades but a master of none? Do others think of you this way? We all have different identities, but sometimes being at the margins of multiple groups can make us feel as though we are perpetual outsiders. A nurse-midwife we interviewed told us, "Sometimes I feel that being both a nurse and a midwife exposes me to the critiques people have about both professions, and at the same time, being both means that I am not sheltered by either because I am always an 'other' inside those groups.

So I often find myself taking the safe route and sticking to practices generally accepted by both."

Left untackled, this fear can limit us: It led the nurse-midwife to temper her professional actions. Resolving this fear requires acknowledging it and diagnosing its cause. Do your multiple identities make you feel vulnerable? Do you worry that one identity may invalidate the other? Do you feel constantly marginal, belonging nowhere rather than everywhere?

Once you have identified the source of your fear, you can begin to contextualize it. When and where does it come up? How is it triggered? How does your fear relate to the relationships between the different groups or roles you belong to? For example, by tracking her own reactions, the nurse-midwife realized that her insecurities came to the fore most often during her shifts with a doctor she perceived as conventional and hierarchical. After further reflection, she realized that the problem wasn't the doctor—who had never actually criticized any of her midwifery-oriented practices—but instead with her fear of being seen as "other." By getting the fear out and understanding it, we can get ahead of it.

Resist either/or thinking about your identities

The default tendency for many of us is to parse our "selves" into smaller, easy-to-define pieces that compete for time and attention. We think, "Becoming an X takes away from my role as a Y." But identities cannot be turned on and off, even though the world sometimes seems to prefer we stay in one tidy box. As an Iranian-American woman told us: "I am not 50% Iranian and 50% American, I am 100% of both." And as Meghan Markle, the biracial Duchess of Sussex, actress, and activist, once told *Elle*: "Being 'ethnically ambiguous,' as I was pegged in the industry, meant I could audition for virtually any role. . . . Sadly, it didn't matter: I wasn't Black enough for the Black roles and I wasn't white enough for the white ones, leaving me somewhere in the middle as the ethnic chameleon who couldn't book a job."[3]

But Markle overcame this, saying, "While my mixed heritage may have created a grey area surrounding my self-identification, keeping me with a foot on both sides of the fence, I have come to embrace that. To say who I am, to share where I'm from, to voice my pride in being a strong, confident mixed-race woman."

Don't pressure yourself into picking just one part of who you are. Having one identity does not automatically diminish another, and trying to turn identities on and off can waste time and energy. Embracing this reality can help you identify connections between your identities that you can then leverage.

Create connections between identities

Don't think about each of your identities as being independent pieces of who you are; think about how they're connected and how they might affect each other in positive ways. One approach is to use a holistic mindset and seek a unifying theme between your identities. For example, in one of our studies we talked to people participating in athletic events that raise money for a charitable cause—for instance, a bike ride for a children's hospital in Israel. One of our participants, an observant Jew and avid cyclist, told us: "It is the perfect confluence of all my passions—biking, giving, and Israel." Other participants described coming to view their multiple identities as a "package" where one aspect of who they were couldn't be separated from another.

To create your own connections, ask yourself *why* your identities are important to you and *how* they relate to one another. For example, a participant in a different study explained that all of his various jobs—IT engineer, journalist, and entertainer—converged around the skill of writing. To find your unifying theme, take a step back from the day-to-day bustle of your roles and find the common ground—their shared skill, meaning, or purpose.

Another approach is to consider how your identities complement each other. For example, one person—a pastor, karate teacher, and yoga instructor—told us about reconciling her jobs into a fulfilling career. "I think Christianity doesn't really tap into the physical part of life. It does deal with the mind aspect and the spiritual aspect," she said. "My definition of a yoga teacher is just someone who helps people to develop a full-spectrum practice in their life. For me, that includes the spiritual/mental/physical, body/mind/soul, the whole person." We heard similar stories from professionals in other industries about how having a variety of distinct roles allowed them to be their fuller selves.

Leverage these connections

Embracing your multiple identities can improve your ability to find creative links between them.[4] Can you take skills learned in one identity and repurpose them in another? Try this framing: "Becoming an X allows me to be a better Y because . . . "

For example, the nurse-midwives we interviewed talked about blending their midwifery and nursing backgrounds to find innovative solutions for their patients. And a chief of radiology, charged with integrating the radiology departments of two merging hospitals, found important synergies between his role identities: "From a managerial standpoint, my role is change management and navigating the hospitals through complex changes. But my clinical background and particularly experience in my area of emergency radiology has been invaluable. . . . The relationships that I developed and working with them in the ER [as a radiologist] were useful in implementing the changes that we're making here."

Connections between work and home can also be influential. We interviewed a designer who was part Mexican and part white and worked on social impact projects. She described being raised in a family that was "incredibly diverse in every single way, socioeconomically, ethnically, educationally"—an experience that helped her "understand people for who they are and not any sort of label which might precede them." She brought this mindset to her work by creating a unique organizational culture at her firm, one that deemphasized the role of the designer as the sole authority and put decision-making power into the hands of her clients.

Change How You Relate to Others

While changing how we see ourselves is a necessary first step, in order to manage how others see and relate to us, we also need to change how we act out our identities. Sometimes relationships in one part of our lives can exert a pull that makes us ignore other aspects of who we are, or they can create challenges that make us feel that it's easier to just be unidimensional. For example, when a working father is asked by his boss to entertain visiting clients at the last minute, he may reluctantly agree, feeling as though he has to suppress his parental identity and commitment in order to be a good employee. You can manage how others see you by finding a balance between your identities, managing your role boundaries, and establishing your authenticity.

Find your balance

You may or may not have chosen the various identities that you hold, but what you do control is how you live these identities. How you structure your time and surroundings will impact your ability to establish and maintain a sense of equilibrium. This balance will look different for everyone.

For some, this might mean devoting yourself completely to one role for a certain period of time and then later turning to your other roles to recharge. Or it can mean spending just enough time on one role to feel nourished, while mostly focusing on other roles. For instance, sometimes it may take an hour of focused writing in the early morning for a budding entrepreneur to feel as though she is moving her side gig forward, and then she can leave for her day job energized and inspired.

For others, balance may mean carefully planning their weeks to ensure they have dedicated time to fulfill each of their roles regularly. A management consultant told us about learning to consider his family members as being as important as clients, in order to help him carve out time for them during his workweek.

Once you establish practices like these, it is critical to communicate them clearly to others, in order to shape their expectations of you, avoid interpersonal conflicts, and get their help in maintaining your priorities. You can also check in with yourself. An individual with four jobs explained to us that rather than measure her "balance" at the end of each day or each week, she took time at the end of each month to assess whether she felt good about how she was allocating her time and energy, and what changes she needed to make for the next month.

Manage your boundaries

Another important step is to manage boundaries in ways that protect each identity while enabling synergy between them. To do this, you need to be socially savvy and flexible. For example, some management consultants developed relationships with colleagues with whom they could be honest about their devotions to both work and family. These colleagues provided emotional and practical support (such as helping them say no to additional work requests) so that they could better maintain boundaries between work and home.

Some people are increasingly using social media to control the boundaries between their identities. For example, one person with multiple jobs uses some outlets (Twitter, LinkedIn) for professional endeavors, and others (Facebook) for personal matters. A journalist we interviewed talked about her complete online separation between personal and professional selves: "Women I've spoken with, we deal with a lot of creepy people . . . so much so that I have changed my Facebook [and made] myself as elusive as possible. You cannot find my name, even though [at] every journalism conference I go to, they say [to] have a public Facebook profile so you can interact with people. I cannot. I've got to protect myself."

Present yourself authentically, but thoughtfully

We all face social pressure to "be authentic." But that does not mean you have to be unfiltered and forthcoming with everything, to everyone, all the time. You can share different aspects of who you are depending on your preferences and the circumstances.

In one of our studies, people with multiple jobs slowly revealed parts of their selves when relevant to their client interactions.[5] For instance, a childcare worker who also ran a nutrition shop only talked about her shop with parents when she felt they could benefit from some nutritional advice for their children.

Biculturals are often adept at "code-switching," or shifting which aspects of themselves come to the fore according to the culture they are in.[6] And people code-switch even within professional contexts. One Wall Street professional told us that she connects different parts of herself with different clients—she could authentically be her Southern "lite" self when she was meeting her clients down in Birmingham, Alabama, and authentically be her New York "full-frontal self" when negotiating in Manhattan.

Create Space for Others' Complexity Too

Thinking about ourselves and our relationships is a crucial first step to thriving with complexity, but to truly change we must also acknowledge others' complexity. To do this, we have to rethink our role models and encourage others to embrace complexity.

Rethinking our role models

Collectively, we need to broaden our narratives about what constitutes success. Our work is governed in many ways by the role models we look up to. Often we portray work heroes as unidimensional, focusing on just one part of their identities and ignoring how other aspects of their selves may have influenced their success.

In her television shows, Rhimes has deliberately built complex and multifaceted characters, with the aim of normalizing all backgrounds and helping our social consciousness move away from the notion of one "right" way to live.

Similarly, we can all work to destabilize the shared narratives we have about what it takes to get ahead. In her book, *Expect to Win*, Carla Harris provides examples of times that mentors helped her to showcase her multifaceted self, such as when one invited her to sing at a work party. Doing so let her connect in meaningful ways with other colleagues and ultimately made her feel like her authentic self at work.

Leaders and managers have an important role to play here in thinking carefully about who is showcased among the team and who is praised. One entrepreneur told us that when introducing guest speakers at the conferences she hosts, she makes sure to weave in interesting facts about the speaker's background and other roles in order to emphasize the person's complexity.

Organizations also share the responsibility of normalizing complexity in the workplace. Leaders can do this by overtly acknowledging individuals as being more than one thing and rewarding different types of performance. For example, one microfinance organization that is dually devoted to advancing a social mission and being commercially viable says employees are both "social workers" and "bankers." To ensure both roles are pursued jointly, it rewards loan officers for commercial success as well as advancing the social mission.

Encourage others to expand themselves

The next step is helping others embrace multiple identities. Leaders and managers should recognize their power in crafting norms and policies that allow (or inhibit) workers' complexity. For example, emerging data from a study we are conducting with elite army officers suggests that most consider "broadening experiences," defined as assignments that force soldiers to engage in roles outside their current functional expertise, to be an essential part of leadership training. In fact, some of the army leaders we spoke with even specify broadening their subordinates' identities as an explicit goal in their leadership philosophies.

In a different context, individuals working at a design firm were told by their supervisors not to work overly long hours, and instead to go out into the world and tap into their other identities. This firm recognized that helping workers to expand their identities enabled them to bring more creative and unique insights to their work.

Most importantly, leaders must embrace their own complexity to ensure others in their organizations will feel it is valuable and safe to do so themselves. Elena Donio, former CEO of Axiom, embraces and openly discusses how she blends her professional and mothering roles in both public and private forums. Our data suggests such displays of complexity matter. For instance, a journalist in one of our studies, after being inspired by another journalist who had revealed his undocumented status, started writing influential articles about immigration issues.

To be effective in today's workplace, we need to shift our mindset and actions from managing oneself to managing one's portfolio of selves. Doing so may initially increase the chaos, but once we fully embrace our complexity, we can feel more fulfilled and create more sustainable and agile organizations and communities.

Adapted from "How to Make Room in Your Work Life for the Rest of Your Self," on hbr.org, May 30, 2018 (product #H04CW0).

4

Why Self-Awareness Isn't Doing More to Help Women's Careers

by Tasha Eurich

Self-awareness is the foundational leadership skill of the twenty-first century. Leaders who know who they are, and how they're seen by others, are more effective, confident, respected, and promotable.[1]

When I speak to business leaders about our seven-year-plus research program on self-awareness, one of the most common questions I get is whether we've found any gender differences.

First, the data: Research has shown that women possess a slight self-awareness advantage over men. In one survey study of 275 people, we found that women's self-ratings of self-awareness are higher (though not dramatically) than men's. Other research has shown that women are rated slightly higher in self-awareness by direct reports as well as managers and peers.[2] Women are also better able to recognize the importance of self-awareness for their career success and advancement.[3]

But despite these advantages, women continue to be underrepresented in senior leadership roles and paid less than men. While gender inequity has wide-ranging causes, focusing on the role that self-awareness plays can give women, and those who champion them, tools to address some of these disparities.

So why aren't women's self-awareness advantages translating into better representation in senior leadership roles? Are there any lessons from the self-awareness literature that could help explain this persistent gap? And what can be done to close it?

Lesson 1: Women underestimate themselves, but not in the way most people believe

It is often said that women are less self-confident than men—yet surprisingly, current findings do not support this idea. Though past researchers documented differences in self-confidence between girls and boys, this gap shrinks dramatically by age 23.[4] And where past research revealed gender differences in self-ratings of managerial effectiveness, more-recent studies have shown that male and female leaders rate themselves similarly.[5]

Yet even though the average woman isn't underestimating herself as a leader, she has a slightly more nuanced challenge: She may not be confident that others value her contributions. In one study, women's and men's self-ratings of emotional intelligence (EQ) did not differ.[6] Yet when women were asked to predict how their supervisor would rate their EQ, their predictions were three times lower than men's, despite being rated slightly higher by their boss than the men were.

Why do women underestimate their true value? Researchers have suggested that persistent stereotypes about leadership's being a male characteristic (whether implicit or explicit) can lead women to worry that they are validating negative stereotypes, which would cause coworkers to see them as less effective than they see themselves.[7]

The ability to correctly predict how others see us, often called meta-perception, is an important aspect of self-awareness. And indeed, when women underestimate how others view their contributions, they may unintentionally hold themselves back. If a female leader believes that others don't value her, she could be more cautious about applying for a job, putting herself forward for a promotion, or asking for a raise.

Therefore, to advance and thrive, women need to gain a more accurate picture of their contributions as seen through the eyes of others. One approach that I often use with my executive clients is the Reflected Best Self Exercise:

1. Identify at least eight people from different parts of your life—current or former colleagues, employees, supervisors, friends, family members, and so on.
2. Send them an email asking when they have seen you at your best. Ask them to include a few specific examples in their response.
3. Review the responses to identify key themes and patterns.
4. Use your findings to compose a self-portrait of who you are at your best through the eyes of others.

The Reflected Best Self Exercise is a powerful vehicle to discover our defining strengths as others see them—something vital for women leaders to understand. It requires a bit of effort and an open mind, but it can help us remove any self-imposed constraints on putting ourselves forward for bigger, better opportunities.

Lesson 2: Women aren't getting good feedback

Feedback is essential if a leader is going to understand her contributions, as well as the adjustments she can make to be more effective. And even though women ask for feedback as often as men, they are less likely to get it.[8]

In my book *Insight*, I tell the story of a client, Eleanor, who was leading a bid for a large water infrastructure program. When her team lost to a competitor, she asked for feedback from a colleague, Phil, to understand her role in the outcome. "You were there during my final presentation," she began. "Did I do anything that could have cost us the work?" Phil replied, "No, not at all. You did a great job." Now Eleanor was even more confused.

A few days later, a colleague called to express his condolences. "It's so frustrating!" Eleanor lamented. "I can't figure out what happened. I know it wasn't my presentation." "Really?" he said. "That's not what Phil told me. He said it was horrible." Eleanor was dumbfounded. She'd gone out of her way to learn what she could have done better, and her colleague had out-and-out lied to her.

Giving honest feedback is notoriously difficult. It can become even more difficult when it crosses gender lines. Researchers have coined the phrase *benevolent sexism* to refer to behaviors that shield women from difficult information. In a work context, male bosses or colleagues may avoid giving women negative feedback because they don't want to hurt or upset them.

When women *do* receive feedback, it's typically less specific than feedback given to men. This has profound consequences: Studies have shown that when women receive vague feedback, they're more likely to be assigned lower performance ratings.[9] Vague negative feedback tells a leader that her performance isn't meeting expectations, but because it doesn't identify the behaviors that aren't serving her, she doesn't know what to do differently.

Vague positive feedback also puts leaders at a disadvantage. It suggests that they are doing well, but because it doesn't point to the actions or results that are valued, leaders don't know what to continue doing. And if they don't have detailed, documented achievements, it's more difficult to make the case for a promotion or raise. When women *can* solicit and record specific positive feedback, it has been shown to effectively eliminate men's overrepresentation in top performance categories.[10]

The question then becomes: How can women obtain more-detailed feedback? In our research with highly self-aware men and women, we discovered an interesting pattern in how they got feedback: They turned to a small circle of people, typically between three and five, who had an active interest in their success and a history of telling the truth when it was difficult. These individuals are ideally at different levels of the organization—one's board members, manager, peers, employees, etc. (For instance, Eleanor's honest colleague would be a great candidate, whereas Phil surely wouldn't make the cut.)

When women leaders can identify and confer with such "loving critics," they can ensure they get the feedback they need. You can formalize the arrangement in whatever way makes sense. One of my executive coaching clients likes to share the behaviors she is working on, then takes each of her loving critics to lunch bimonthly to get their feedback. Another has a slightly less formal arrangement: After a meeting with one of her loving critics, she asks for a two-minute feedback download.

When it comes to the feedback conversations themselves, if they're imperfect at first, it doesn't mean they won't be valuable. Tuck School of Business professor Ella Bell Smith suggests that if feedback isn't specific enough, women should ask follow-up questions like, "Can you give me an example [of] when I did that?" "What was the impact you saw [of that behavior]?" or "How often have you seen me doing this?"

Lesson 3: Women tend to take feedback to heart

Of course, no one should take every piece of feedback at face value, nor should they over-rely on others' views to construct their self-concept. In general, there are three types of information we use to form a picture of who we are: how we see ourselves, how others see us, and comparisons we make with others.[11] While men place more importance on their self-views and social comparisons, women tend to be more focused on how others see them. What's more, even though men and women possess similar views of their performance in the absence of feedback, women are more likely than men to modify their self-views in the presence of it.[12]

Granted, it isn't wise to ignore all feedback from others, but it can be just as dangerous to discount our self-views. Placing greater importance on others' evaluations of our performance can cause us to ignore our own standards and goals, which could make our behavior less consistent with our values. When we become overreliant on others' approval, we may ruminate more on our fears, shortcomings, and insecurities. (And yes, women do tend to ruminate more than men.)

Self-awareness isn't one truth—it's a complex interweaving of how we see ourselves and how others see us. In fact, these two perspectives have been shown to capture different aspects of who we are. For instance, we usually understand our motives better than others do, but others typically see our behavior more clearly than we do.[13] So even though we should take others' opinions seriously, they shouldn't define us or completely override our self-image.

To overcome the tendency to rely too heavily on others' views, women can develop their own picture of who they are. Reflecting on these questions can help:

- What are the principles by which you want to live your life?
- What are your greatest aspirations?
- What types of projects give you the most energy?

No matter what form this reflection takes (journaling, mindfulness, conversations with loved ones, etc.), it's important to prioritize it just as much as feedback from others. (If you want to assess the strength of your self-views—and see how they compare to others—you can take our free, five-minute self-awareness quiz at www.insight-quiz.com.)

Women leaders can often benefit from an extra dose of self-reliance, especially when others can't yet see what we're capable of. So if, for example, you receive negative feedback from your boss on something you think you could excel at, don't give up right away—think about what it would take to show them otherwise. As Supreme Court Justice Sonia Sotomayor once said on NPR's *Fresh Air* podcast, "In every position that I've been in, there have been naysayers who don't believe . . . I can do the work. And I feel a special responsibility to prove them wrong." It never hurts for us to do just that.

Adapted from content posted on hbr.org, May 31, 2019 (product #H04Y39).

SECTION TWO

Show Your Leadership Potential

5

Seeing Ourselves as Leaders

A conversation with Muriel Maignan Wilkins and Amy Jen Su

Making the transition from being one of many on a team to being a leader is a process—not just of convincing other people to see us as leaders, but also of convincing ourselves that we can and should lead. And that can be especially difficult for women.

In this conversation, *Women at Work* cohosts Amy Gallo and Nicole Torres explore the process of becoming a leader, including the soul-searching that women often have to do to get there. They talk to experts on leadership Muriel Maignan Wilkins and Amy Jen Su, founders of the executive coaching firm Paravis Partners and coauthors of the book *Own the Room: Discover Your Signature Voice to Master Your Leadership Presence*.

AMY GALLO: Do you remember the first time that you were seen as a leader?

MURIEL MAIGNAN WILKINS: It was my first supervisory job. Looking back now, I was naive, very young, and thrust into this role supervising individuals who were far more experienced than I was. And while I knew that I was there as a supervisor and as a manager, I certainly didn't see myself as a leader—but everybody else did. It took a couple of big fails for me to step into the leadership role and recognize that it was much more than just making sure that people were doing what they were supposed to be doing. In hindsight, I probably remember it a little bit more painfully than I'd like to.

AMY G.: How about you, Amy Su?

AMY S.: There was a day when I really lost it on somebody who worked with me, and later when I debriefed with that person, I realized how much I was able to cause a bad day for somebody else. There was just this moment of, *Wow, perhaps I'm a leader now, and my temperament, mood, and state of being are actually going to impact the way others feel.*

AMY G.: It sounds like for both of you it was not very positive. It's a bit like an awkward growth spurt to go from someone who's an individual contributor to someone who's now seen as a leader. Is that how you think of it in your writing and your work with coaching clients?

MURIEL: I never quite thought of it as awkward, but certainly an uncomfortable phase, which, as we all know, is where most of the growth happens. It's hard because, on the one hand, you want to go back to what you are comfortable with and what has made you successful up until now. On the other, you know that you can step into the role that you're currently in with the potential that you have. So it's certainly uncomfortable, and it can be awkward. At the same time, it's one of the inflection points that is great for growth for anyone.

NICOLE TORRES: I can think of two challenges that make this such an uncomfortable phase. The first is whether you see yourself as a leader. The other is if you see yourself as a leader, but other people do not. Maybe you've stepped into a managerial role or maybe you're leading a project, and you see yourself as being the one making decisions, but you don't feel like other people perceive you that way. Do you see those two challenges play out?

AMY S.: Muriel and I have definitely seen both sides of that equation. There's your own shift internally around realizing that you are a leader, and that you are bringing a different business judgment and a different set of decision-making skills to the table. At the same time, as you mentioned, it's also interesting to see how perception follows along with that. In our coaching work, we've seen that the internal shift often happens sooner and with a greater pronouncement than how others view you.

AMY G.: Let's take each of those in turn, because while the internal one may happen more quickly for many people, especially women, it is hard to make that leap. When you coach clients, what are the major obstacles, and how do you help them?

MURIEL: In anything, the internal piece is the harder part. But it's also the one that is most sustainable in terms of achieving the transformation, change, or shift that you want to make, whether it's in your career or even in your personal life.

With clients, one of the big things they need to embrace is that being a leader or acting as a leader doesn't necessarily require the hierarchical position. A lot of them wait till they get the promotion—until they're the vice president or managing a team—assuming that that's when they need to be "leaderly." In reality, you should be preparing for this from day one.

With women, part of the challenge is that they are not necessarily conditioned for leadership positions, so they don't get a ton of practice before they enter the workplace. If you look at the research even around young girls raising their hands in a classroom, you start seeing that dissonance very early on.

So a lot of what we work with clients on is not just the mindset in terms of seeing themselves as a leader—what does that mean, how do they want to lead, how do they want to be known—but also starting to understand that there are some specific skills that help in terms of establishing and asserting your leadership. These skills are primarily your communication skills. That includes your ability to speak up, listen, and ask good questions; how you lead your work and drive your work; and even your physical presence with how you hold yourself in a room and a conversation, and whether you do it in a way that makes *you* feel like you're a leader and makes others feel like they're in the presence of a leader as well.

AMY G.: Many women receive messages that in order to be a leader, you need to use typically masculine traits. One of the most popular articles we've ever published on hbr.org is about why so many incompetent men become leaders, and much of that article is about how we value confidence and assertiveness. For some women—myself included—the hesitancy to step into the role in the way you're talking about is like, *Do I have to do that? Do I have to be assertive, aggressive, and authoritative to be a leader?* How do women get over that hurdle?

MURIEL: That is a big, life-affirming question, because the struggle and the tension is between what the world expects you to be and who you are. Even this concept of leadership looks one way, which is, quite frankly, the white masculine way.

From my standpoint, in working with women, the goal is to get them to understand that it is a myth—that the real work starts from within, with understanding who you are and what you stand for. What are your principles? What is your way of being in the world, and which behaviors make you who you are?

Then it's getting them away from what their default behaviors and skills might be—again, how they've habitually created who they are right now and how they act—and get them to think about what they want. The minute that a client says with real conviction that they do want to lead, that's actually the biggest breakthrough. Because they have to own it. Once we understand that, then we can work backward to say, "All right, so how do you do this in a way that supports who you are, while at the same time being relevant and resonating with those who you need to lead?"

NICOLE: Are there specific examples of things that you tell clients who come to you and say, "I want to lead"? What do you tell them to do to establish themselves as leaders if they don't have the title but want to start embodying a leader?

AMY S.: The word "embodying" is really important. We could tell somebody all we want that *I'm a leader, I'm a leader, let me tell you, I'm a leader*—but it's really about the felt experience of the other person.

For example, you might be somebody who historically has asked a lot of questions or asked for advice from others. Maybe in the past I would say to you, "How do you think I should price this proposal?" Instead, in a leader stance, I might come to you now with what I call "the comment and the question," where I'm sharing with you my business judgment first and then asking a question. I might say, "I'm thinking we should price this proposal this way. I think it inherently keeps the value of our firm and at the same time mitigates risks on renewals. But I really value your perspective. Do you think I'm missing anything here?" There's a big difference when our stance is, "Wow, I don't have the answers, so I'm going to go ask others and follow" versus "I'm a leader, I'm going to share with you my judgment, but then be open to other perspectives."

MURIEL: Then, if I can add to that, if a client is working in a specific organization that has its own model of what it looks like to be an effective leader, at a very practical level I ask them, "Do you know what it means to be an effective leader in this organization?" If the answer is no, then they have to go on a little field trip to HR and ask, "What does the leadership model look like here? Is there one?" It's usually made up of 8 to 12 skills, and we start working on those skills.

AMY G.: We probably have listeners who are saying, "I've nailed the internal, I know I want to be a leader, I've looked at the competencies, I've started exhibiting the behavior—but people around me still don't see me as a leader." Do you have any advice for women in that situation, where they feel like they're pushing to be a leader, but they're not getting the response they want?

AMY S.: The word you use, "pushing," really says a lot. When we are coming from a place of trying to prove ourselves, people can smell that, and there's a tremendous amount of insecurity that sits underneath it. So, there's a distinction for me between "I really own my expertise and understand the business knowledge, skills, and experience that I bring to the table" and "I need to prove that I'm an expert, and I hope they see me as an expert." Somehow, folks can tell the difference. We need to push ourselves to ask, "Is the pressure to prove I'm an expert actually getting in the way?"

MURIEL: It's important to also bring people along. Many times, individuals are not pushing back on you trying to grow and spread your leadership wings, if you will. The issue is that they're not used to it. They're used to operating with you and experiencing you in the way that you have been. It's helpful to have a couple of advocates, champions, and sponsors who are excited for you to spread your wings, and who you rely on in terms of getting advice, counsel, and mentoring as you're going through this passage. That way they are coming along with you.

For women in particular, depending on where they are in their career, this is especially important. I've seen many women get caught up in a sort of father/daughter relationship when their manager or their mentor is a male. Is that really the dynamic that you want to have, whether it's conscious or unconscious? Bringing people along—being very explicit that you want to grow as a leader, that this is your intent as you go into that next position, and asking for their support—can be healthy in moving through that transition.

AMY G.: You also have to be specific, because if you say to your manager, mentor, or sponsor, "I want to be seen as a leader," that could mean a zillion different things.

MURIEL: Yes.

AMY S.: Absolutely.

AMY G.: So you need to say, "I want to be able to make the decision on X. I want to be someone who people seek out for expertise on Y." You need to be more specific and, as you say, Muriel, make a request of, "Here's how you can help me do that."

MURIEL: Right. Ask in a specific way. Seek counsel and say, "Manager, I really want to work on my ability to be seen as a leader. Six months from now, what would be some of the hallmarks that you'd expect from me if that's my goal?"

AMY G.: I once noticed that someone who many people thought of as a leader often said at the end of the meeting, "Let me know if you want me to weigh in on that." And I was like, "Oh, I should use that." That's a good line because it demonstrates *I have expertise, and I'm willing to help if you want my opinion.* It was such a nice way to establish leadership without having to say, "I'm in charge."

AMY S.: You're mentioning something here that does distinguish a leader. You begin to see at more senior levels that people are just more comfortable batting ideas around with each other in a peer-to-peer way. Often you can see that somebody is still trying to make that turn, because they're still walking in with the overpackaged document or overpackaged presentation, and they feel like they can only speak when it's about their area. Part of being seen as a leader is the willingness to bring your judgment, bring your acumen, and talk about things in a much more informal way.

AMY G.: I was asked a question recently by a Black woman who said that she worked in an organization where she just felt like she was never going to succeed because of her race and her gender. She said, "How do I know when it's just not going to happen, where I'm not going to be seen as a leader because of these biases, versus because I haven't done enough yet?" Do you have advice for someone in that situation?

MURIEL: I would look at the signs that she's getting. Number one, when she looks ahead of her in terms of the different ranks, what does that look like? Are there any other women or people of color or—bingo, bonus—women of color that are more senior? Is there a track record there?

Secondly, is she getting support even in the role that she's in? Is she being offered, even if she has to ask, opportunities to get not only visibility but also more experience and exposure? Because those are the things that will actually get you ahead. It's the visibility, the social capital, and the knowledge capital, which only come through experience. If she's getting knocked down every time she asks, well, then that's another sign. The other question is, can she find a sponsor, even if it's an informal sponsor within the organization?

Let's assume her performance is really top-notch. What I would say is, if you're able to do everything that you can in these areas that I spoke of, and over time it doesn't seem like it's leading to anything, then you do need to have a frank conversation with yourself around whether this is the place that's going to set you up for success in terms of the goals that you want. You also have to ask yourself what your time limit is. Everybody's timing is different. I do think that some people opt out too early, but you need to set a time range. And sometimes you don't really know till you go elsewhere.

NICOLE: I know we all have those moments of doubt. But if you start seeing yourself as a leader, and you sense that other people doubt you—maybe they think that you have progressed too fast or they still see you as someone who needs training wheels—how do you preserve your own sense of confidence so that you know you *can* lead and some people are just wrong about you?

MURIEL: One of the things that is helpful, particularly when you take on a management role for the first time and you start leading a team, is to—very early on—get on the table what people's hopes and aspirations are in terms of you being the leader. But also understand what their concerns might be. That ability to listen to the concerns gives you an added advantage in terms of being able to not get defensive and address them. And hearing what the expectations are, so you can start being in tune with those expectations and get some quick wins, starts building your credibility. My biggest warning is to not get defensive. If you get defensive, it's just going to alienate everyone, and you don't want to be in that position.

AMY G.: What if you're not sure if you want to lead? How do you decide whether this is something you want to do?

MURIEL: This is where you really need to think through what the next couple of years look like for you. I don't think it's a lifetime decision. Some people look at it as, "What do I want to do with my life?" I suggest looking at things in a three-to-five-year horizon. Five years seems like a very long time to me. Focus on the next couple of years rather than the rest of your life: What are the different scenarios? Which ones are more aligned with what you want?

What you don't want to have happen is to follow a particular scenario out of fear. That's a very different way of opting out. I remember early on in my career, I recognized that I was getting very close to being able to gun for partner at a consulting firm. While I believed that I could do it, the question was, did I want to? Those are two very different things. So, the first question is, do you think you can do it? The second is, do you want to? I recognized after a lot of my own soul-searching, talking to others, and looking at those who are ahead of me—even those that I greatly admired—that it was not what

I wanted. And the reason I didn't want it is that it wasn't the way that I wanted to make an impact.

So having the ability to sit back and think about those two questions—do I believe I can do it and do I want it—is critical.

Adapted from "Seeing Ourselves as Leaders," Women at Work *podcast season 4, episode 10, December 16, 2019.*

6

Act Like a Leader Before You Are One

by Amy Gallo

If you want to become a leader, don't wait for the fancy title or the corner office. You can begin to act, think, and communicate like a leader long before that promotion. Even if you're still several levels down and someone else is calling all the shots, there are numerous ways to demonstrate your potential and carve your path to the role you want.

What the Experts Say

"It's never foolish to begin preparing for a transition, no matter how many years away it is or where you are in your career," says Muriel Maignan Wilkins, coauthor of *Own the Room*. Michael Watkins, the chairman of Genesis

Advisers and author of *The First 90 Days* and *Your Next Move*, agrees. Not only does the planning help you develop the necessary skills and leadership presence, but it also increases your chances of getting the promotion because people will already recognize you as a leader. The key is to take on opportunities now, regardless of your tenure or role. "You can demonstrate leadership at any time, no matter what your title is," says Amy Jen Su, author of *The Leader You Want to Be* and coauthor of *Own the Room*. Here are several ways to start laying the groundwork.

Knock your responsibilities out of the park

No matter how big your ambitions, don't let them distract you from excelling in your current role. Focus on the present as much as—or more than—the future. "You still have to deliver results in your day job," says Su. Adds Wilkins, "You always need to take care of today's business so that nobody—peers, direct reports, or those above you—questions your performance." That's the first step to getting ahead.

Help your boss succeed

"You have to execute on your boss's priorities too," says Watkins. "Show her that you're willing to pick up the baton on important projects." Wilkins also suggests you "lean more toward yes than no" whenever your boss asks you to help with something new. Find out what keeps your manager up at night, and propose solutions to those problems.

Seize leadership opportunities, no matter how small

Make sure your "let me take that on" attitude extends beyond your relationship with your boss. Raise your hand for new initiatives, especially ones that might be visible to those outside your unit. "This will give others a taste of what you'll be like in a more-senior role," says Wilkins. It doesn't have to be an intense, monthslong project. It might be something as simple as facilitating a meeting, offering to help with recruiting events, or stepping in to negotiate a conflict between peers. You might find opportunities outside of work, too. You can sit on the board of a local nonprofit or organize your community's volunteer day. "These activities send the signal that you aspire to leadership potential," Watkins says.

Look for the white space

Another way to prove your potential is to take on projects that others aren't willing to tackle or don't even know exist. "Every organization has needs that nobody is paying attention to, or that people are actively ignoring," Wilkins says. For example, you might be able to identify

How to Improve Your Leadership Presence

BY MURIEL MAIGNAN WILKINS

Presence. You know it when you see it—and you notice when it's missing. It seems to come so naturally to some people, like a CEO who can own any room or a leader who has great charisma. Yet for a lot of people who'd like to develop their own executive presence, it's hard to know where to start.

I've worked with hundreds of clients, and I find it helps to break executive presence into three essential areas that you need to work on together:

- **Set the right assumptions.** Before your next meeting, think about who will be there and what they hope to get out of it. The mindset you bring to the table will shape every interaction you have. Assumptions can set you up for success or undermine your best efforts before you even open your mouth. Leaders with presence are honest about their assumptions so that they are not ambushed by them.

a customer need that isn't being met by your company's current product line, and propose a new one. Or you could do a quick analysis of how much a specific change would save the company. When you take on a task that no one else is willing to do, you make yourself stand out.

- **Review your communications repertoire.** These are the tools and techniques you use to engage, influence, and inspire other people. Quite simply, they're how we try to get our points across. Some people use humor, others ask questions. Some people give clear instructions, others might frame them as suggestions. Ask yourself which communication strategies you tend to use in different situations.

- **Manage your energy.** Your energy sets the tone for any interaction. It's not as easy as remembering to stand up straight or stop frowning. You need to match your energy to the situation. To learn what kind of nonverbal cues you're giving off, film your next presentation or meeting or ask for feedback from a mentor.

Developing leadership presence does not need to be a mystery. Break it into manageable pieces by focusing on your assumptions, your communication strategies, and your energy.

Adapted from "Improve Your Leadership Presence" (video), on hbr.org, April 16, 2013.

Don't be a jerk

There's a fine line between being ambitious and acting like you're too big for your britches. "Don't try to exert authority when you don't have it," says Watkins. Practice what he calls "steward leadership": Focus on what your team wants to accomplish instead of putting yourself first. Su recommends "humble confidence," showing appropriate modesty in your role while having the self-assurance to know that you will rise to the next level. (See the sidebar "How to Improve Your Leadership Presence.")

Be cautious when sharing your ambitions

It's appropriate to raise your ambitions with your manager if you have a trusting, solid relationship, but frame them in a way that focuses on what's best for the company. Su suggests you lay out your accomplishments for the past year and then ask something like, "As we look further out, where do you see me continuing to make a contribution?" Watkins warns that these conversations shouldn't come off as being all about you. Instead, engage in a two-way conversation with your boss. And if you have the kind of manager who may feel threatened by your aspirations, it's better to keep your ambitions quiet and prove your potential.

Find role models

Look for people who have the roles you want and study what they do—how they act, communicate, and dress.

"Pick someone at the next level, someone similar to you, and find a way to work with them," says Watkins. Volunteer for a committee they're spearheading or offer to help with one of their pet projects. Identify behaviors that you can emulate while being true to yourself. "You don't want to fake it," says Wilkins. It might also help to study people who are stuck in their careers as examples of what not to do, Watkins says. Are they clumsy politically? Do they disrespect the lines of authority? Do they fail to make connections between departments?

Build relationships

There's an old adage: "It's not who you know, it's who knows you." When you're evaluated for a promotion, it's unlikely that your boss will sit in a room alone and contemplate your potential. She'll rely on others to assess your ability, which means you need supporters across the organization—people who are aware of the work you're doing. "If you find yourself walking down the hall with the most senior person at your company, be prepared to answer the question, 'So what are you up to?'" Wilkins says. "Don't take lightly any interactions that may seem informal. Treat every situation as an opportunity to demonstrate the value you bring to the organization and your knowledge of the business."

Case Study: Focus on Solving Problems, Not Getting Promoted

In late 2010, after 10 years at Citi, Heather Espinosa was promoted to managing director. She reached this executive position by continuously challenging herself—and by making the most of each of her previous roles. "I've never been concerned with my title. When I thought an assignment was a stretch, I took it," she explains. "When I applied for my previous position, the job carried the title 'project manager.' But after my first conversation with the manager, I knew it was a position that would require complex leadership skills and challenge me, so I accepted the job."

In each role, Heather embraced additional responsibilities without being asked. "I make an effort to volunteer and raise my hand where I see a need. I started taking on the responsibility of managing director with the hope that if I performed well, the title would come." And her bosses have always respected this approach. "I rarely walk into my manager's office and say I want to talk about my career or my next promotion. I walk in and say, 'Here's a problem, and here's how we might address it,'" she says.

Adapted from content posted on hbr.org, May 2, 2013 (product #H00AK9).

7

How to Increase Your Influence at Work

by Rebecca Knight

To be effective in organizations today, you must be able to influence people. Your title alone isn't always enough to sway others, nor do you always have a formal position. So, what's the best way to position yourself as an informal leader? How do you motivate colleagues to support your initiatives and adopt your ideas? How can you become a go-to person whom others look to for guidance and expert advice?

What the Experts Say

Having influence in the workplace has "clear value," says Dorie Clark, author of the book *Entrepreneurial You*. "You get more done and you advance the projects you care about and are responsible for," which means "you're more likely to be noticed, get promoted, and receive raises." But gaining influence in the modern workplace is difficult, according to Nick Morgan, author of *Power Cues*. "It's never been harder to influence others, because they've never been more distracted," he says. "Information overload and the pace of our digital lives have [led to short attention spans]." And yet, "it's more important than ever to be able to command influence, because of the increased pressure on getting results." It all comes down to your approach. Here are some tips.

Build connections

It's not quite a junior high school popularity contest, but "at a fundamental level, one of the reasons that people do things for you"—support your idea or approve your budget—"is because they like you," Clark says. You don't have to be "the awesome-est person in the room" or make sure "everyone is blown away by your charisma." You just need to have a good rapport with your colleagues. This won't translate directly into influence, of course, but it does "make it more likely that others will at least hear you out." Work on cultivating personal connections with your colleagues, and allow them to get to know you. "That way, they won't impute negative intentions or motives to you."

Listen before you try to persuade

The best way to prime colleagues for backing you and your agenda is to make them feel heard. Start by giving them your undivided attention in one-on-one situations. "Most of us walk around with a running to-do list in our heads," Morgan says, and it shows. We're fidgety, preoccupied, or ready to reach for our phones. Instead, you should "practice the discipline of focus." To do this, "turn your body toward the other person, freeze in place, and listen." Clark agrees: "A big part of workplace resentment is people feeling disrespected and that their voices aren't being heard." So, ask colleagues for their perspectives and advice.

Mind your body language (and your tone)

People are constantly assessing whether to trust you or not, Morgan says. "[We're] hardwired to be asking the question, 'Is this person a friend or foe? Is this person trying to undercut me, or are we on the same side?'" Your body language is critical to conveying the right message. Standing up straight with your shoulders back helps you come across as confident and commanding; slouching and looking down at your feet has the opposite effect. "When you adopt a certain [slumping] posture, you think in subordinate terms and you talk in subordinate terms, and it increases the likelihood that you'll be seen as less authoritative," Morgan says. For instance, imagine that you have a meeting with a colleague you don't know well from another division. Morgan suggests signaling that you are a friend by keeping your arms uncrossed, your hands by your sides, and "your torso open and pointed at the other person." He also advises "pitching your voice a little lower than you normally do" to connote power. "This is useful to work on because it counteracts the effect of nervousness, which tends to push your tone higher."

Develop expertise

Another way to increase your influence at work is to "be seen as a recognized expert" within your industry or organization, Clark says. This won't happen overnight, but you can take steps to develop business-critical expertise and know-how. She suggests "immersing yourself in your topic area" by regularly attending industry conferences, enrolling in a class or specialized certification program, or taking on a leadership role in a relevant professional organization. "Those are visible and public signs" that you are staying up to date and informed, she says. Don't keep your knowledge under wraps. "Blogging about your subject on LinkedIn or for your company newsletter" is another way to show what you know.

Map a strategy

When it comes time to leverage the influence you've built to promote a particular initiative or idea, be strategic. Clark recommends creating a "power map" to guide your campaign. "Create an org chart of decision makers related to your issue," she says. As you go through the levels, "ask yourself, 'Can I influence this person directly? If not, whom can I influence who can influence that person?'" Then begin to think about how and when you will approach these various colleagues. "War-game the situation," she says. "Who might be threatened by your plans, and how can you bring them over to your side?" You're not scheming; you're strategizing.

Give people what they want

You can increase your influence on a particular issue by authentically framing it as a benefit to the people you want on your side. Consider each stakeholder's needs, perspectives, and temperaments. "Do your homework to find out what they need to hear and what will capture their attention," Morgan says. For each person, "make sure you're answering the question, 'What's in it for me?'" He also recommends talking about how an idea will "benefit the organization" as a whole. "Use the word 'we,' as in, 'We'll see value,'" he says. Clark concurs: "If your proposal is fundamentally self-interested, people won't line up."

Case Study: Build Relationships with Your Colleagues

Marcy Shinder, chief marketing officer at Work Market, the New York City–based firm that helps businesses manage their freelancers and consultants, was working on establishing herself as an influential member of the team before she even started the job.

Before her first day of work, she arranged to meet several colleagues for informal coffees and lunches—one-on-one meetings that were "more personal, less structured, and allowed us to establish rapport." "I went in with a listening agenda," she explains. "I wanted to learn: What are their goals? What is important to them? What do they think is working at the company? And what do they want me to accomplish?"

Marcy made sure her body language conveyed that she was fully focused on these conversations. She sat up straight, made eye contact, and looked open and engaged. "Body language is so important—we coach salespeople on it," she says. "I tried to listen with intent."

Those early meetings allowed her to understand the perspectives, personalities, and motives of her colleagues, which proved to be useful when she had an idea to revamp the company's website and needed their support to move forward.

Thanks to those early one-on-one conversations, she could customize her pitch to each individual. For example, with Stephen Dewitt, the CEO, she talked about the company's vision. With Jeff Wald, the president and COO, an analytic thinker, she started with the metrics. And with the chief customer officer, she focused on the customer side.

"It is the same story, just with a different emphasis," she says. Her efforts paid off. The new Work Market website went live the next spring.

Another way Marcy increases her influence is by staying up to date on industry trends and news. "I spend 25% of my time talking to customers, other chief marketing officers, people on boards of companies, and potential customers, and on mentoring young people," she says. "By doing that, I stay informed and I have a finger on the pulse of what's happening beyond the four walls of this company."

Adapted from content posted on hbr.org, February 16, 2018 (product #H046D5).

8

Why You Need an Executive Voice

by Rebecca Shambaugh

Whether you are an associate manager or a senior executive, what you say, how you say it, when you say it, to whom you say it, and whether you say it in the proper context are critical components for tapping into your full strategic leadership potential. If you want to establish credibility and influence people, particularly when interacting with other executives or senior leadership, it's important to be concise and to let individuals know clearly what role you want them to play in the conversation. It's also important to demystify the content of any message you deliver by avoiding jargon and being a person of few—but effective—words.

All of these factors relate to developing a strategic executive voice. Your executive voice is less about your performance than about your strategic instincts, understanding of context, and awareness of the signals you send in your daily interactions and communications. Like its sister attribute, executive presence, executive voice can seem somewhat intangible and thus difficult to define. But the fact is, we all have a preferred way to communicate with others, and doing this with strategic intent and a solid grasp of context can mean the difference between success and failure in your communication and leadership style.

One of the most important aspects of having an executive voice relates to being a strategic leader. I frequently hear from top executives that they would like to promote one of their high-potential leaders but feel the person is not strategic enough to advance. When I hear managers say this, I try to gently push back and suggest that maybe the problem isn't the candidate's lack of strategic leadership potential; perhaps they are failing to tap into their abilities as a strategic leader.

Whether you think someone on your team lacks strategic readiness or you're worried that *you* might have untapped strategic potential, read on. Below are some coaching strategies that I use frequently with both male and female executives to help them add a more strategic executive voice to their leadership tool kit.

Understand the Context

How often do you find yourself throwing out an unformed idea in a meeting, not speaking up when people are looking for your ideas, or saying something that doesn't quite fit the agenda and suddenly getting that "deer in the headlights" feeling? If these situations sound familiar, what is it that went wrong? In short, these types of tactical errors come down to failing to understand the context of the call, meeting, or discussion that you are in.

For example, if you are the primary authority on a topic, then it's likely that the context would require you to lead the meeting and make any final decisions. But if you are one of several executives who might have input, then sharing your view and connecting the dots with others (rather than stealing the spotlight with your great ideas) would be your role. If you are in learning mode and are not asked to present at a meeting, then your role when it comes to communication would be to observe and listen. Knowing or finding out in advance what your expected role is in a group forum or event can guide you. Use that information to determine the kind of voice you need for that particular venue, and to help ensure that you understand the context before you speak up.

Be a Visionary

Sometimes we fail to tap into an executive voice because we focus too much on our own function or role. Strategic leaders are more visionary than that, taking an enterprise view that focuses less on themselves and more on the wider organization. Another part of being visionary is developing the ability to articulate aspirations for the future and a rationale for transformation.

This type of executive vision helps guide decisions around individual and corporate action. You should work toward connecting the dots with your recommendations to show how your decisions affect others around the table, including your staff and the organization as a whole.

Cultivate Strategic Relationships

One of the best ways to build your strategic thinking is by leveraging relationships more intentionally, with specific business goals in mind. This calls for having senior leaders and executives who bring a strategic perspective of the organization's goals, changes, and top priorities that normally we may not have access to. When you cultivate and invest in broad strategic relationships, it helps you avoid getting caught up in day-to-day minutiae.

It's easy to lose sight of the significance of cultivating new and diverse relationships when you already have a full plate. But part of finding a strong executive voice is expanding your knowledge beyond your specific position, department, or area of expertise.

To develop your executive voice, take time to reach out to at least one person each week outside of your immediate team or functional area. Try to learn:

- How they fit into the business as a whole
- Their goals and challenges
- Ways you might support them as a strategic business partner

Bring Solutions, Not Just Problems

While coaching a wide range of executives, I've seen firsthand that most feel frustrated when people point out challenges but don't offer any resolutions. Leading strategically with a strong executive voice involves solving problems, not just identifying difficult issues.

You can show up more strategically by doing your homework and taking the lead in analyzing situations. Brainstorm fresh ideas that go beyond the obvious. Even if you don't have the perfect answer, you can demonstrate your ability to come up with clever solutions.

Stay Calm in the Pressure Cooker

People with an effective executive voice aren't easily rattled. Can you provide levelheaded leadership even when—in fact, particularly when—everyone around you is losing their composure? When you can stick with facts instead of getting swept into an emotional tailspin, no matter how stressed you feel, you'll be able to lead with a more powerful executive voice.

It can be uncomfortable to recognize personal challenges regarding your executive voice, and at first you may get pushback when making suggestions to improve the voices of those on your team. But once you overcome this initial resistance, whether in yourself or others, you'll find it's worth the up-front effort to investigate how to contribute most effectively to important meetings and other communications. By making the necessary adjustments to your approach to participation, you can start showing up more strategically in every setting.

Adapted from "To Sound Like a Leader, Think About What You Say, and How and When You Say It," on hbr.org, October 31, 2017 (product #H03ZDX).

9

Make Yourself Sponsor-Worthy

by Sylvia Ann Hewlett

Maggie says, "I've always given 110%. Whoever I worked for, I gave them my all, every day, 10 hours a day, weekends and holidays, whatever it took. That endeared me to a lot of powerful men."

That dedication and loyalty should have made Maggie a star. Yet although she rose in the organization, because she wasn't strategic about whom she gave her 110% to, she squandered her gifts on leaders who didn't invest in her. Without a sponsor to spotlight her attributes, offer her opportunities, and kick her career into high gear, she found herself stuck in what she calls "permanent lieutenant syndrome."

Eventually, Maggie was fortunate enough to find a sponsor, and today she is an executive at a global financial advisory firm, with 22,000 people reporting to her. But there are thousands of Maggies out there—hardworking, devoted, consistent performers toiling in relative obscurity. How can you break out of the pack and attract a sponsor?

Rather than hoping for a lucky break, focus your energies on making yourself sponsor-worthy. To begin with, you must come through on two obvious fronts: performance and loyalty.

When asked how she built great relationships with three different sponsors, Sian McIntyre, head of legal at Lloyds Banking Group, says simply, "I've delivered." Her *performance* helped her stand out. She hit her targets and deadlines, executed brilliantly on her assignments, and produced outstanding bottom-line results. "They all felt the benefit of that," McIntyre notes, "and wanted me on board for subsequent projects."

Loyalty manifests in the trust that's earned through repeated demonstration of work ethic, commitment to a shared mission, and allegiance to the firm. Winning a sponsor's trust doesn't require becoming a toady. On the contrary, showing that you can ultimately be entrusted with a leadership position depends on demonstrating that you will stand up to a superior when necessary.

Tiger Tyagarajan, CEO of Genpact, attributes his success to the bond he cultivated with Pramod Bhasin, his boss and sponsor for 17 years. Because of a deep trust built on shared values, Bhasin would listen when Tyagarajan pushed back. "I'd say, 'Here's my logic on this,' and show him that I understood his logic but also show him why it wouldn't work. He was amenable to that as long as I kept it private," Tyagarajan recalls. "We had very different styles, and sometimes we simply agreed to disagree. But in the end, I think that what he valued in me was the very thing that complemented him."

Yet performance and loyalty are not enough to get a sponsor's notice, let alone convince them to invest in you. You'll need to differentiate yourself from your peers. You'll need to develop and deploy a personal brand. You'll need to do *something* or be *someone* who can extend a sponsor's reach and influence by adding distinct value.

What Do You Bring to the Table?

Some protégés add value through their technical expertise or social media savvy. Others derive an enduring identity through fluency in another language or culture. Consider acquiring skills that your job doesn't require but that set you apart—and make you a stronger contributor to a team. For example, Tyagarajan had a special ability to build teams from scratch and coach raw talent—an invaluable asset as the firm transitioned from a startup into a multinational infotech giant.

One 25-year-old sales rep, noting her potential sponsor "wasn't exactly current in terms of the internet," took pains to brief her on job candidates whose résumés were packed with technical jargon and references to social media innovation that she simply couldn't understand, let alone assess for relevance. "I just helped educate her so she didn't come off as some kind of dinosaur," says the rep, whose tactful teaching gained her a powerful promoter.

Lastly, don't be shy about your successes. Alert potential sponsors to your valuable assets. Since it can be difficult to toot your own horn, work with peers to sing each other's praises. A vice president at Merrill Lynch described how she and three other women, all high-potential leaders in different divisions of the firm, would meet monthly for lunch to chat about their projects and accomplishments. The idea was to be ready to talk each other up, should an occasion arise. "So if my boss were to complain about some problem he's struggling to solve, I could say, 'You know, you should talk to Lisa in global equities, because she's had a lot of experience with that,'" this vice president explained. "It turned out to be a really effective tactic, because we could be quite compelling about each other's accomplishments." In short order, all four women acquired sponsors and were promoted.

Finding the Right Sponsor

When scanning the horizon for would-be sponsors—and yes, you need more than one—be strategic. Efficacy trumps affinity; you're looking for an ally, not a friend.

Your targeted sponsor may exercise authority in a way you don't care to copy, but it's their clout, not their style, that will turbocharge your career. Their powerful arsenal includes the high-level contacts they can introduce you to, the career-advancing stretch assignments they can help you land, their broad perspective when they give critical feedback—all ready to be deployed on behalf of their protégés.

Look beyond your immediate circle of mentors and managers. While you should, of course, impress your boss—who can be a valuable connection to potential sponsors—seek out someone with real power to change your career. Would-be sponsors in large organizations are ideally two levels above you with line of sight to your role; in smaller firms, they're either the founder or president or are part of their inner circle.

Finding the right person to highlight your accomplishments and push you to the top is a hard task, but it's necessary if you want to break out of the "permanent lieutenant" doldrums. Just doing good work isn't enough. Take the first step and make yourself not only a hard worker, but an emerging leader worthy of a sponsor.

Adapted from "Make Yourself Sponsor-Worthy," on hbr.org, February 6, 2014 (product #H00NIB) and "The Right Way to Find a Career Sponsor," on hbr.org, September 11, 2013 (product #H00B7X).

SECTION THREE

Advocate for Yourself

10

The Art of Claiming Credit

A conversation with Amy Jen Su

Long before you get recognized for a great idea, you have to say what that idea is, often in front of a group. These are those moments when we sense that what we're about to say and how we say it might affect how our colleagues see us, and whether our idea is going to go anywhere.

In the following conversation with *Women at Work* cohosts Amy Bernstein, Nicole Torres, and Sarah Green Carmichael, Amy Jen Su explains how women can put their ideas out there—and get proper credit. Amy is a managing partner and cofounder of the executive coaching firm Paravis Partners, coauthor of *Own the Room: Discover Your Signature Voice to Master Your Leadership Presence*, and author of *The Leader You Want to Be: Five Essential Principles for Bringing Out Your Best Self—Every Day.*

NICOLE TORRES: What are some clues that you're not getting the credit you deserve for the good work you're doing?

AMY JEN SU: Here are a few scenarios you may encounter. You're in a conversation with somebody, and you think you're working on something significant, and somehow you sense that others are surprised—as if they are taken aback that you're doing something bigger than they thought you were capable of. If you're starting to sense that from your key stakeholders, that's definitely a clue.

If you start to feel like your career is stalling out, or that you're burning out, those are two important places to pause and ask yourself, "Why am I being passed up for certain opportunities?" or "Am I so exhausted because I'm just doing, doing, doing, and not getting the credit for it that I deserve?"

NICOLE: If you are in that situation, how do you change that artfully?

AMY S.: It begins with the way you prepare. Oftentimes we have the faulty assumption that we can just wing it. So before any important meeting, high-stakes situation, or instance where you're going to be visible, make sure you're prepared enough that you can look like you're reacting on the fly. Have some nuggets in your back pocket so that you can speak in real time, and give thought to how you can drop in ideas or share what you're working on. What are three to five things that you are excited about?

Part two of that preparation is to make sure that you're artful in considering your audience. Who's going to be in the room? Who am I speaking to? What do they care about? Make sure that you're framing accordingly. For example, if I said, "Hey, guess what—I talked to five customers this week," what's your reaction?

SARAH GREEN CARMICHAEL: If we hadn't been talking about anything else, it might seem out of nowhere.

AMY S.: Right. Sometimes when we think, *Oh, I'm trying to find that perfect moment to drop in and get credit for something*, it can feel like it's out of left field for other people. I might instead say, "You can't believe the trend I've been hearing this week out in the marketplace. I spoke to five of our top customers, and all of them reported that our competitor is starting to cut prices to get market share. Maybe we should call a meeting to talk about this as a team."

SARAH: That's so much better. There's a point to it. There's a call to action or a reason for you to share that.

AMY S.: Right. So when we say "claim credit," it's not out of the blue, with no context. Instead, I'm looking for those moments where I'm lifting up and out of the noise of my work and saying, "How can I add value? How can I share about something I've learned that actually helps to move the business forward?"

AMY BERNSTEIN: How do you know that the person you're talking to—your manager, your manager's manager—is actually open to hearing this? It seems like some people are, but then there are some people who just aren't interested in credit, one way or the other.

AMY S.: Boss dynamics are tricky. I think the other arsenal in our tool kit then would be "shaping questions." Sometimes there are folks who'd rather hear themselves speak—they aren't great listeners. But we can still show up with tremendous presence and show our critical thinking by asking questions. For example, sometimes we can get too short-term or operationally focused on the activities of today, instead of having a dialogue with our boss or others around shaping what success looks like: What do benchmarks tell us? What are our options here? What are the risks and trade-offs? Try to draw them into the dialogue and make it a two-way thing.

SARAH: I got some advice early in my career: "You'll be amazed by how much you get done if you stop caring about getting credit and just let other people think it's their idea. You'll be able to have a lot more influence." Where do you come down on this continuum—claiming credit versus letting other people think it's their idea?

AMY S.: It's really a balance. You should think about it more in terms of taking responsibility and ownership for your work and ideas, making sure that at every moment you're demonstrating your ability to strategically inform and be comfortable in your visibility. When we're claiming credit, we're really trying to make sure that the organization and our teams are leveraging us as highly as possible. For those reasons, it's important to find a way to do it that feels authentic. At the same time, it is important to also be a team player and to know when to pick those spots.

But I've seen many of my clients have an allergic reaction to claiming credit, because it can be so confusing. In fact, I've had some clients say to me that they feel angry about it, because it feels like they're being asked to be political or Machiavellian. So we just need to make sure that we're not framing claiming credit as bragging or self-promotion. Instead, it's remembering to take ownership of our work and being willing to show courage in our convictions.

SARAH: When you talk about claiming credit, it sounds less like a reactive response and more about owning your space. Why do you think of it that way?

AMY S.: Whenever we're reactive, it can feel like you're backed up on your heels. It can feel defensive. I prefer to work with folks around what offense looks like. As you walk through the world confident and clear on what you're doing and the difference you want to make, and informing people and sharing your contributions in a way where you aren't holding yourself back, in many ways—just inherently—credit is coming more than it would be in that more reactive, defensive posture.

NICOLE: Research has found that women get less credit than men for the same work, but women also get less credit when they're working with men on the same projects. If you are a woman finding yourself working with mostly men on something, what can you do to set yourself up so you are getting your fair share of credit?

AMY S.: If you find yourself in that situation, first make sure to be proactive rather than reactive. The key thing to keep in mind is, "Am I making the clear requests that I need to along the way?" For example, one of my clients is co-leading a project with a male colleague who has a very strong and dominant personality. She's had to be very clear and say, "Hey, it would be great to be included on those sets of calls," or "Make sure you send me the agenda in advance, and I'll add my thoughts to it," or "Let's talk in advance about who's going to lead what part of the agenda, so we're a united front." So that's the first tip: Be proactive versus reactive.

The second is that, as women, we need to be more comfortable in and aware of space. And that comes in many forms: Maybe it's when you walk into a conference room, not being shy about picking a chair that's in the flow of the conversation, or even at the head of the table if you're one of the co-leads. Maybe it's being mindful of your volume, depending on the size of the room. Maybe it's making sure your voice gets out there in the early part of the meeting so that you can be heard. Oftentimes, people notice if you can hold your boundaries, and if they sense that you can't, they will take your share of air, and they will interrupt you.

AMY B.: Let's say there's someone whose recognition you'd like to have. How do you have a follow-up conversation with that person without feeling icky and gross?

AMY S.: That one's tough, especially when you've been in the presence of somebody you aren't around often, and you didn't fully share what you were hoping to share. To avoid the ick factor, pause and ask yourself, "Is this the right time? Was there something in the information I was hoping to share, or that I wish I had shared, that would be beneficial or important to the other person?" If the answer is no, you might just let it go. If the answer is yes, check the person's calendar and make sure they're showing an open block. Then just pop into their office and say, "Hey, that was such a great meeting. The point you raised about X or Y got me thinking about some additional information that might be helpful to you." Then share that piece of information. But I do think there's some discernment needed on whether to do that at all.

NICOLE: If the best course of action is to let something go, how do you avoid feeling resentful or discouraged that work you've put in is not going to be recognized?

AMY S.: I hope one of the takeaways on this topic is, we all need to stop beating ourselves up. So number one: self-compassion. We're not always going to get this right.

With lots of these situations we've been talking about, there's retrospective awareness, where we're realizing something after the fact. Then we move from just realizing it to saying, "I don't want that to become a trend or pattern. How do I get in front of it? How do I change the way I prepare for another situation down the road, so that doesn't happen again?" Over time, we move from retrospective awareness to prospective awareness, to being able to—in the moment—find that right moment and put it out there.

Adapted from "The Art of Claiming Credit," Women at Work *podcast season 2, episode 6, October 22, 2018.*

11

Get Yourself Invited to Important Meetings

by Nina A. Bowman

In a work culture with too many meetings, we often look for ways to get out of meetings. But sometimes you need to get *into* a meeting, perhaps because the decisions made there will have implications for you or your team, or maybe because you feel you've been left out of important discussions. Whether you haven't been invited because of an oversight or an intentional decision by the meeting organizer, you can take action to secure your seat at the table.

But First, Pause

Despite all the talk about decreasing the number of meetings we attend and the importance of having only the key people in the room, let's face it—there are times that not being on the invitation list can sting. Intellectually, you may understand the logic, but that's little consolation when you want to be included. It may hurt even more when you realize that an invitation snub sends a signal to your team and colleagues, who may wonder, "Why isn't our boss in that meeting? Is there a shift of power happening in the organization?" Before making any moves, think objectively about whether you *really* need to be in that meeting. Ask yourself:

- Am I a decision maker on the topic?
- Will I or my team be significantly affected by the outcome?
- Do I bring knowledge or information that others don't have?
- Do I bring a unique perspective that isn't already represented?

If you answer "yes" to any of these questions, then start the process of understanding why you don't have an invitation.

Assess Your Value

The real currency of a consistent seat at the table is value. If the meeting organizer has left you out, they may not understand what value you bring to the discussion.

Take one of my clients, whom I'll call Mark, as an example. He is the assistant director of a contract research organization. Mark's boss was leading meetings to discuss restructuring the research business and hadn't been including Mark on the invites. Mark felt that he not only should be invited but should be leading the meetings. He wondered whether his voice was appreciated. When Mark finally mustered the courage to inquire about the situation, he learned that his boss felt frustrated that he had to lead the meetings, which he was doing only because he felt Mark wasn't stepping up with ideas and a process for moving the restructuring forward.

Mark was surprised. He saw himself as a key decision maker, but he hadn't been acting like one. In an effort to not step on toes, he had been deferring to his boss on the restructuring—but his passive approach was undermining him. If he wanted to regain his boss's trust, he would need to prove his value. Only then would he be able to get a seat at the table, and even take over leadership of the meetings.

Assess Your Style

You may have been left out of a meeting because of the way others perceive your behavior.

Take another client of mine, whom I'll call Karen. She was on the legal compliance team at a fast-growing biotechnology company. Her role was to work with marketing to ensure that promotional campaigns and materials were in line with government guidelines. Karen had always been invited to key marketing meetings, but she noticed that more and more meetings were happening without her. In fact, she was not brought into the discussion until campaigns were far along in their development and it was too late for her to influence the marketing team's decisions. The pattern was starting to create blowups between the legal compliance team and the marketing team, since Karen was forced to unravel significant marketing campaigns late in the game.

When I spoke with Karen's marketing colleagues, they told me that they found her presence in meetings frustrating. They respected that her role was to help manage the company's legal risk, but she had a tendency to shoot down ideas and take a conservative stance on gray areas, leaving the marketing group feeling demoralized. The team wanted Karen to listen openly, brainstorm along with them, and focus on solutions instead of problems. When Karen heard this feedback, she realized that while she brought unique knowledge and information to the meetings, her style was preventing others from seeing that value.

If you've been left out of a meeting, consider asking your peers for feedback on your style and making the necessary shifts so that others can appreciate what you bring. Karen worked on listening actively and made a point of proposing a solution—not just naming the problem—whenever she identified a compliance issue.

These changes made her a better business partner to her marketing peers and helped her get back on the invite list for those meetings.

Use the Right Strategy for the Situation

Securing an invitation to an important meeting will likely require different tactics depending on the situation. Here are tips for some of the common situations I've seen my coaching clients face.

Your boss goes to all the meetings and leaves you out

- Set aside time to talk with your boss about your goals and interests.
- Directly state your interest in attending specific meetings, and ask what you can do to demonstrate your value.
- Ask your boss if there are projects you can work on that would help you be included in those meetings.
- If your boss agrees that you should be included in future meetings, don't be bashful about reminding them about that commitment. For example, you might ask, "Would the upcoming strategy

meeting be an appropriate time for me to share the new competitive analysis research I've been working on?"

A peer is intentionally excluding you

- Set up a time to have a conversation with your peer about the pattern you're observing.
- When you explain why you should be in those meetings, focus on the business reasons, not your personal interest or feelings.
- If you continue to be left out, ask someone who is invited (and whom you trust) to send an email to the organizer, ideally cc'ing the other participants encouraging your attendance. Your colleague might say something like, "Juan, I think Katie's perspective in this meeting will be helpful to the group. We should consider adding her to the meeting." That way the decision isn't up to the peer who has been leaving you out.

You just aren't on the organizer's radar screen

- Start by asking yourself whether you are spending enough time developing strong relationships with your coworkers. Getting to know your colleagues increases the chances that they'll be more aware of your work and the value you might bring to their meetings.

- If there's a specific meeting you're targeting, make clear to your manager that you're interested in joining and ask for advice on what you can do to be included.
- Proactively share with the organizer how your work aligns with the goal of the meeting.
- Make yourself useful. Share relevant information with the meeting organizer and offer your assistance. For example, you can say, "Céline, I know that you have an upcoming meeting to discuss the new account strategy. I thought you'd find this information useful. If it would be helpful, I'd be happy to come to the meeting to discuss the implications with the group."

In any of these situations, it may be that you weren't left out of the meeting intentionally. Making clear that you're interested in attending and explaining the value you can bring can often remedy an oversight.

When you're not invited to a meeting, it's easy to blame others for excluding you, but that typically won't get you the invitation. Ultimately, the responsibility is yours to prove why you should be in the room.

Adapted from "How to Get Yourself Invited to Important Meetings," on hbr.org, May 7, 2018 (product #H04B0C).

12

Having the Here's-What-I-Want Conversation with Your Boss

by Rebecca Shambaugh

One person stands between you and your next raise or promotion: your boss. While others on the leadership team—and even your peers—may exert some influence on your career, it's your direct supervisor who can pull the strings to either grant or deny your advancement. But to get what you want, you have to ask for it.

I once spoke at a conference in New York, where a female executive pulled me aside to ask my advice on this topic. She explained that while she was on the verge of being promoted to the C-suite, her family situation with three children had many demands. She was feeling conflicted about whether or not she could take on higher-level responsibilities while remaining both a strong professional and a strong parent. In confidence, she shared with me that she was planning to resign from her position and company later that month.

I then asked her a question: "Did you consider going to your boss and directly asking for what you want—maybe some additional time off or even going part-time for a while—to facilitate your ability to accept the promotion while still making more time for family?" My point was that when it comes to your career, whether your goal is a promotion, a raise, or something else, it doesn't have to be all or nothing—if you learn how to identify what you want and confidently ask for it.

At its core, the act of asking your superior for something important to your career progression may make you feel vulnerable—yet summoning the courage to do so actually demonstrates strength. Whether you seek more money, higher status, increased visibility, additional resources, or more time off, you likely won't get it if you don't specifically ask your boss for it. What's more, many bosses *expect* you to directly ask for what you want. Asking shows both self-confidence and respect for your manager, since you are requesting, not just expecting, help.

Assuming that you've already done your prep work—researching your case and your company's policies and financial position—here are a few tips on actually having that conversation with your boss.

Avoid assumptions by asking the right questions

Successful negotiation is about not just asking for what you want, but also approaching your "ask" strategically. A poor strategy is to approach negotiations one-dimensionally, focusing only on your own desired outcomes. Instead, you should take a collaborative approach, building a clear bridge between your boss's concerns and your request. The best way to do this is to pose a few open questions that explore your boss's view of the world. When formulating these questions, be curious about how to make your request a win-win. For example, you might try using phrases that imply joint success, such as:

- How do we both do well?
- How would you define success?
- How can we turn this into a win for you?

However, in keeping your boss's perspective in mind, be careful not to spend too much time listening passively or go overboard with the questioning. The key is to find the perfect balance between listening and asking questions, ultimately steering the discussion toward an answer.

Gather context through open dialogue

Getting the lay of the land directly from your manager before asking for what you want can help you formulate a better strategy. Initiate an open dialogue tailored to the specific points you plan to negotiate. For example, if you're targeting a promotion, you might ask something like this: "Now that I've been in this role for two years, what actions would it take to advance to the next level?"

This type of question can spur your boss to reveal valuable information to guide your future negotiation. For example, your boss may tell you that there is currently a freeze on promotions but it's an avenue that can be explored in six months. In this case, you'll then know that the timing is wrong to negotiate for a promotion right now—so you can shift gears to ask for something else, or pose other questions to gather the information you need to get what you want down the road. For example, some questions you might ask include:

- Assuming things are different six months from now, what are my chances of gaining a promotion?
- What specifically do I need to do to achieve this goal?
- Are there stretch assignments that I can take on over the next six months to prepare me for advancement?

Then follow your boss's guidance, and commit to revisiting the topic in six months for a reevaluation of the timing.

Use "what if" responses

One way to build on your boss's responses during the open dialogue stage is to have some "what if" responses ready to go. "What if" responses give you a way to further the conversation by suggesting specific actions that you might take when your boss makes a general suggestion. For example, if your boss says that you need more cross-functional experience before you can advance, you might reply with an exact strategy that you could implement to get that experience, such as:

- What if I work directly with the marketing department on the Johnson campaign?
- What if I take the lead in sharing our communications strategy with the sales team?
- What if I shadow the distribution team lead for a week, or participate in a one-day role swap with a peer in the finance department?

Involving your boss in your request by using the "what if" tactic will help gain their buy-in and commitment with a tangible plan that can be tracked and monitored.

Let the conversation evolve

Even if you execute a perfect ask, there may be circumstances beyond your control that cause your boss to reject your request. Don't become so fixated on achieving your ultimate goal that you leave possible chips on the table. Keep an eye out for viable backup plans that emerge as the conversation unfolds. Even if you get a "no" to your original request, you can still leave the negotiation with a small win that may put you on the path to an eventual "yes." Your goal should be to avoid ending up in a position where the response is a final "no."

For example, say you ask for a salary bump, proving through your internal and external market research why you deserve one, and your boss responds that there's currently no budget for raises in the department. You might then shift the conversation to requesting an extra week of vacation, more flexibility in your job, a benefit option, or paid continuing education in an area that supports your career goals.

Even if you accept a plan B as a result of your current negotiation with your boss, that's no reason to give up completely on what you really want. If your manager denies your request the first time, it doesn't necessarily mean that "no" is the final answer.

No matter your perceived level of expertise in negotiation or the style you use to go about it, there is power in simply moving beyond your nervousness and starting a conversation with your boss about what you want. By doing so, you'll begin to build both your skill level and confidence, preparing you for future negotiations.

While you may not get what you want every time, if you don't ask, you'll never know.

Adapted from content posted on hbr.org, November 20, 2015 (product #H02IBL).

13

How Women of Color Get to Senior Management

by Cindy Pace

Women of color are a force in the U.S. economy. They are projected to make up the majority of all women by 2060, which means they'll also likely become the majority of the U.S. workforce. They also generate $1 trillion as consumers and $361 billion in revenue as entrepreneurs, launching companies at four times the rate of all woman-owned businesses.[1]

Developing a diverse leadership pipeline can benefit companies in all sectors. Firms with the most ethnically diverse executive teams were 33% more likely to outperform their peers on profitability, and those with executive-level gender diversity worldwide had a 21% likelihood of outperforming their industry competitors.[2] A 2018 study of VC firms found that more-diverse teams had higher financial returns than their homogenous counterparts.[3]

The problem is that, to date, companies have not been great at promoting women of color to senior roles. And this isn't for lack of ambition among them: According to Lean In and McKinsey & Company's "Women in the Workplace" report, Black women are even more likely to aspire to hold a powerful position with a prestigious title than white women are. And yet Black women's advancement into leadership roles has remained stagnant, even as the number of them in professional and managerial roles has increased.[4]

To increase diversity at senior executive levels, more must be known about one group in particular: women of color in midlevel leadership, who successfully developed and progressed beyond individual contributor and first-line management. What made their ascent possible? How did (or didn't) managers play a role? And what factors helped or hindered advancement in their organization?

To look into these questions, I conducted a case study as part of my dissertation research involving 23 women of color at a *Fortune* 500 company.[5] Sixteen women were interviewed and seven others participated in a focus group. The participants were American women whose racial and ethnic identity was African American/Black, Asian American, Latin/Hispanic, or any combination of these. They were employed in midlevel and upper-midlevel management positions in strategy, finance, marketing, legal, operations, and technology functions. Each had been employed for at least two years and had aspirations to move into executive management or senior leadership. They had all received at least one promotion or expansion of roles and responsibilities within management at their present company, and had been identified as having high leadership potential.

How to Get Ahead

The women in my sample were asked to think back on two defining career moments that best prepared them to advance. What were the critical events, and what lessons did they learn?

My analysis of the women's responses, including their career decisions and the support they received from their managers and organization, led me to identify four main ways they developed and advanced toward their goals:

They aspired to power and influence

It might seem obvious, but the women in my sample had high ambitions to hold executive leadership roles with high status, power, and influence. This aspiration served as a motivator for them in making trade-offs to progress into top leadership, which could include anything from making a lateral move to changing companies to working long hours.

Navigating Intersectional Invisibility

BY ALEXIS NICOLE SMITH, MARLA BASKERVILLE WATKINS, JAMIE J. LADGE, AND PAMELA CARLTON

Black women continue to be sorely underrepresented in leadership roles in corporate America. Yet, despite this underrepresentation, a small subset have found success as leaders and played key roles in driving organizational change. We conducted in-depth interviews with 59 Black women executives across various industries who have occupied senior-level positions in U.S. corporations.

Our findings indicate that one main driver of their success was their ability to navigate the challenge of *intersectional invisibility*, or the tendency to be overlooked, disregarded, or forgotten due to one's status as a member of two underrepresented and devalued groups.[a] To adapt to this invisibility, they employed different strategies based on their career stage.

Early Career: Self-Awareness

As they first grappled with feeling both visible and invisible at work, the women we interviewed said they developed a keen awareness of their unique, albeit disadvantageous, position. Despite this, these women were resilient and learned to craft their professional identities to align with others' expectations for potential leaders. This often meant scrutinizing their appearance, style, and character, and carefully constructing professional images to help them "blend in" and disconfirm negative stereotypes.

Mara, a senior vice president in a pharmaceuticals company (all names have been changed to protect the interviewees' privacy), told us, "I was Black, they were white . . . I was female, they were all male. . . . There was nothing that was an obvious similarity between us. I think I spent my early years trying to mask how different I really was." For instance, every Sunday night Mara would memorize sports scores just in case she had to talk to someone about them.

Of course, in trying to mask their gender and race, many of our interviewees felt a diminished sense of authenticity that became emotionally taxing and costly. Mara eventually gave up on feigning interest in sports. Instead, she began focusing on building relationships with colleagues based on shared interests and experiences such as family and travel. "Nobody can accept and like me if they don't know me," she said.

Mid-Career: Strategic Risk-Taking

Research suggests that women and minorities are often tested in leadership roles by being disproportionately given risky or precarious assignments, a phenomenon referred to as the "glass cliff."[b] Although the glass cliff tends to be positioned as negative, most of the women we interviewed viewed risky roles as

(continued)

strategic opportunities to overcome their invisible outsider status and prove their worth as leaders.

Some women had to fight others' low expectations of their skills and abilities. Pilar, an executive vice president in consumer products, told us that her glass-cliff roles helped disprove the executives who thought she wouldn't be able to handle the job: "I felt it bought me some organizational credibility."

Those who opted out of risky assignments did so primarily when it violated their personal values and beliefs, or when they assessed that they lacked the necessary resources and support for success. Fear of failure was not central to their decision making. In other words, rather than saying, "I can't do that," the women in our sample were more likely to say, "I won't do that." In such cases, they were likely to leave their organizations.

Senior Level: Hypervisibility for Impact

By the time they reached the apex of their careers, the women told us, they sought to have impact in hypervisible ways. In addition to achieving career success as leaders in their organizations including a few attaining C-suite positions, many of them reached beyond their day-to-day responsibilities by taking on additional organizational roles such as championing diversity and inclusion efforts, joining boards of other (frequently nonprofit) organizations, and mentoring the next generation of diverse leaders.

Rather than hiding their unique status, they chose to be authentic leaders and share their experiences with others—particularly up-and-coming Black associates. Sarah, a senior vice president in financial services, said: "It is about creating the environment, the safety net, and the opportunity to institutionalize some things . . . so that the next generation of folks who pass through here, who are likely to be younger, more diverse, ambitious . . . if they work hard, and we create the kind of environment for them to be their best self, the company will do extraordinarily well, and by extension so will they."

a. Valerie Purdie-Vaughns and Richard P. Eibach, "Intersectional Invisibility: The Distinctive Advantages and Disadvantages of Multiple Subordinate-Group Identities," *Sex Roles* 59 (2008): 377–391.

b. Michelle K. Ryan and S. Alexander Haslam, "The Glass Cliff: Evidence that Women are Over-Represented in Precarious Leadership Positions," *British Journal of Management* 16 (2005): 81–90.

Adapted from "Interviews with 59 Black Female Executives Explore Intersectional Invisibility and Strategies to Overcome It," on hbr.org, May 10, 2018 (product #H04BBI).

They also understood the reasons behind their ambitions and used these reasons to drive them. Some women wanted to advance to senior leadership roles so they could influence business strategy, lead change, and advance the goals and values of the company. Others wanted power in order to bring out the best in their teams and foster an inclusive culture.

They confidently seized opportunities

Transitioning from first-line leader to midlevel leader required women to believe in their ability to perform across a variety of situations, identify and seize opportunities, and promote their capabilities and interests. Acknowledging their desire for advancement and seeing themselves as leaders allowed them to step outside their comfort zones to raise their hands for assignments, acquire skills, and take roles beyond their area of expertise. This allowed them to explore unfamiliar functions and business units to gain experiences that were new, difficult, and uncomfortable.

Bianca (all names have been changed), an assistant vice president (AVP), described seeking opportunities in areas outside of her expertise:

> *There's one thing I've learned about how to take steps to get to where I want to be: I must take chances and risks by learning about areas that I don't know about.*

Lisa, another AVP, let it be known to the leaders in her organization that she was interested in working in Latin America. As a result, she was offered a leadership role:

> *I've always been interested in working internationally, and so I put it out there. I'm now an AVP in Latin America, learning Spanish, and have respon-*

sibilities for a team of 12 to 14 people and an entire line of business. There are opportunities that I now have in this role that I may not even have had the opportunity to experience if I had stayed in the United States.

Other women described working in areas outside their current expertise, allowing them to learn product areas or skills as part of their leadership growth.

They pursued management challenges

The developmental experiences that best prepared the women I studied (and this is likely true of other aspiring leaders as well) were challenging management experiences that offered broader leadership responsibility and greater business scope. In order to advance from first-level management toward senior leadership, the women in my sample needed to have access to managing people, critical negotiations, new businesses ventures, and external client relations. These situations involved complex assignments focusing on strategy, product development, business operations, and financial management. The women started small, but started somewhere, and then increased the complexity over time.

These experiences were especially important in workplaces undergoing rapid organizational change, and served as important tools for women of color to elevate their skills.

Astrid, a sales vice president (VP), described a staffing experience from very early on in her career that taught her the importance of understanding a team's culture before making changes that affected her employees:

> *I was the manager of a call center, and I inherited all of my team. I had a very diverse team with a very different and strong culture. I came in as a go-getter and directive leader, thinking I was going to implement some meaningful change. I was extremely ambitious and extremely independent. This was a very family-oriented community that viewed their work as a means to pay for their life with their family. It was a huge lesson for me in that, as a leader, [I had to] learn the culture.*

Adriane, another VP, reflected on having to make an unpopular decision. In her organization, there was debate about whether their associates should change managers. After hearing feedback from all across the world, she chose to have employees change managers, even though it was unpopular among some. She reports it "was a hard decision to make, but it felt like it was the best decision for the organization."

A third VP shared about taking on a new and unfamiliar experience of leading an entire financial team, bringing in new leaders, and outlining a plan to grow the organization.

They cultivated influential mentors

Having influential senior leaders—including men as well as women of color—serve as mentors, advisers, and role models provided emerging women managers with the tacit knowledge needed to navigate their company's leadership structure. Mentors also advised on some of the less-talked-about necessities for staying on a desired career path: boosting resilience, coping with difficult emotions, and managing hypervisibility (the experience of feeling constantly observed because of one's difference, or of feeling "on display" as one of the few women of color in the company).

For the most part, the women I studied had to take the initiative to build strong relationship capital across identities and throughout the organization. Women who were savvy in this area described receiving career advice, psychosocial support, and growth opportunities through the developmental relationships they fostered with senior leaders, former managers, and influential mentors in their network.

That said, some reported being approached by leaders in their organization. Laura, a VP, noted that a leadership team member sat down with her to talk for more than a half hour during her first six months on the job.

"Since then," she reports, "I've consistently had interactions with our leadership team members and eventually ended up working for the same senior leader, who is now a direct report of the CEO, who came into my office years earlier."

Blythe, an AVP, shared that her managers are women and are big on empowering their associates. "Having the opportunity to present to senior leaders would not have happened if they didn't actually allow me to have a seat at the table for the discussions," she notes.

The Organization's Role

Elevating women of color isn't just the job of the women themselves, as these experiences highlight. Yes, women as well as men must be intrinsically motivated to aspire to leadership roles and seize opportunities. But companies also have a key part to play in fostering diversity in their leadership pipeline. Here are some steps they can take:

Educate managers about the work realities faced by women of color

Women of color face barriers that many other employees don't. Their credibility is often questioned; they're stereotyped and seen as token employees; they aren't afforded access to critical leadership experiences; and they are often excluded from influential networks. (See the sidebar "Navigating Intersectional Invisibility.") Managers need to understand how and why these women face these challenges, including the emotional tax they face for being different, and come up with solutions to combat them.[6] To begin, leaders can make inclusion visible and part of the company's core values. Secondly, they can embed inclusive behaviors and practices into employee and manager development. (See the sidebar "How Pinterest Empowers Inclusive Leadership" for an example of how one company does this.)

This said, training alone will change nothing if managers aren't held accountable for culture and talent. Business leaders monitor and are held accountable for making or missing sales goals, so why not the same for diversity and inclusion? That's why companies must monitor culture and talent metrics for women of color (hires, promotions, turnover) in addition to surveying them about how they're experiencing their development and progression (or lack thereof). Companies should also openly acknowledge and celebrate inclusive managers in public workplace communications. In addition, to support managers, they can create forums where managers can be vulnerable, talk about mistakes, and ask questions.

How Pinterest Empowers Inclusive Leadership

A CONVERSATION WITH CANDICE MORGAN

Candice Morgan is the former head of inclusion and diversity at Pinterest, where she worked to improve the company's diversity rates and create a more inclusive culture. In this brief conversation, Women at Work *cohost Nicole Torres talks to Candice about how she encouraged inclusivity at the managerial level.*

NICOLE TORRES: One of the things you're focusing on is training managers to be more inclusive. What are you doing specifically?

CANDICE MORGAN: We did an internal study where we looked at our managers and tried to understand the differences between the ones who scored exceptionally high on inclusion, as rated by their employees, and the ones who got average scores.

There were a number of things that those exceptionally inclusive managers were doing. They valued employees' ideas even when those ideas differed from their own, and they were more willing to admit their mistakes, which creates safety for taking risks and being able to grow, learn, make a prediction or mistake, and come back from it. Those managers also spent more time soliciting feedback from people around what they want to work on, and found ways to make those passions a part of employees' roles. They invested more in structured socializing and ensured the socializing was inclusive for everyone—not after work with a beer, but much more broad and intentional.

These exceptionally inclusive managers did these things naturally. They also had a humility to them, which brings up the idea of being authentic. If you can admit your mistakes, you signal a type of trust and authenticity to your employees. We created a playbook based on those inclusive behaviors, and we now have all new managers go through this inclusive manager training and use that playbook as a resource.

NICOLE: It sounds like by training managers to be more aware of themselves and to be more authentic themselves, that helps employees also feel like they can be their real selves at work.

CANDICE: Yes. Sometimes leaders will ask, "What's the most important thing that I can do?" It's modeling that authenticity. It's being able to talk about the times you made a wrong call and what you learned from it. That encourages other employees to do the same.

Adapted from "Lead with Authenticity," Women at Work *podcast season 1, episode 3, February 9, 2018.*

Integrate conversations on workplace biases into sponsorship programs

Sponsorship has been identified as an important yet underused tool for affirming aspiration, unlocking potential, and driving engagement in employees of color.[7] When sponsorship works, it can provide the support and advocacy needed for advancement. However, to develop trustworthy connections, sponsors and protégés must be able to openly discuss negative stereotypes, microaggressions, and challenges or barriers that women of color face in the workplace. This, of course, can be difficult or uncomfortable. So before pairing sponsors with protégés, it's vital that both sponsors and high potentials are prepared to be advocates and allies.

Sponsors should be formally trained on topics such as minimizing unconscious bias, developing inclusive behaviors, valuing differences, and understanding power and privilege in corporations. And protégés should be trained on how to be sponsor-ready by giving them background information on the unwritten rules of senior leadership, strategic stakeholder management, and authentic leadership presence.

Ensure women of color's access to essential business experiences

Exclusionary cultural practices are often deeply embedded in company culture, organizational structures, and talent practices. For example, one study revealed that there are gender and racial disparities to work assignments.[8] These types of disparities often shut women of color out of the critical business experiences they need to advance in leadership. In traditional male-dominated hierarchies, tacit knowledge about how the organization works, what advancement opportunities are available, and how to access mentors and sponsors is often shared through homogenous closed social networks that women of color aren't privy to. How can women raise their hands for opportunities if they don't even know these opportunities exist in the first place?

To improve upon this, companies need to make women of color's access to highly visible and critical business assignments a strategic priority. One approach is to invite them to shadow executives, which can help demystify leadership and provide an understanding of the business challenges leaders face. Women should then be given access to sponsors (if they haven't already) to ensure this shadowing isn't a one-time event, but is part of a long-term commitment to their learning and advancement.

Women of color aspire to hold top leadership roles that allow them to lead with influence and purpose. Too often, their ambitions are thwarted. But learning from women of color who have advanced can help other women and the companies they work for turn aspirations into something more concrete: meaningful and long-lasting leadership experiences.

Adapted from content posted on hbr.org, August 31, 2018 (product #H04IKM).

14

Advance in Your Career, Even When Your Boss Won't Help

by Kristi Hedges

I once moderated a panel at a conference and asked the group of successful executives to describe someone who has been instrumental in their careers. Two panelists eagerly jumped in with stories of bosses who had mentored, encouraged, and opened doors for them. Then, hesitantly at first, the last person shared a far different experience.

She lamented that she'd never been lucky enough to work for someone like that, and at times felt that the lack of an effective boss was career-derailing—even a personal failure. At one point she had worked for a leader who started to coach her but was then replaced by someone with such a lack of political savvy that she learned to do exactly the opposite of whatever he advised. Eventually she figured out that instead of waiting for a boss who could advocate for her, she had to create a workaround.

As she spoke, I noticed how many people in the audience were nodding their heads, and afterward she was flooded with questions.

A sponsor can be invaluable for achieving your career goals and getting ahead in an organization. The first place we all look for an advocate is our immediate boss, the person who is closest to our work. A good advocate offers advice and mentorship while also shining a light on our potential—revealing capabilities that we may not know we have. We borrow an advocate's confidence in us until we adopt it fully ourselves. One of the panelists recounted a story of how his boss shocked him by suggesting him for a job before he was ready. He took it, and with his boss's close guidance, learned as he went.

Sponsors also serve as role models, allowing us to see how we can accomplish what they've done. (This is one reason representation is so critical to changing the gender and racial imbalances in companies.)

But in my experience, it's uncommon to have a career-supporting advocate in our direct manager. Supervisors too often lack people development skills or organizational influence. Or they are too protective of their own status to risk elevating someone else.

So what should you do if you're not one of the lucky ones with a powerful boss who supports you? First, know you're in good company: The playing field isn't as uneven as you may think. Second, use the following advice to find what your boss isn't giving you.

Create an Advocacy Team

Instead of having one person in your corner, consider putting together a team of people who can help you advance your career. Think broadly across levels and functions, both inside and outside your organization. Look for people whose careers are further along than yours and whose style or achievements you admire. It can help to write the qualities you want to develop and match them with a list of people who exhibit them.

A graceful way to approach a potential advocate is to ask for advice. Rather than showing inadequacy, asking for advice makes people seem more credible, according to research from Harvard Business School and the University of Pennsylvania's Wharton School.[1] Further, when people provide advice, they become invested in it, and therefore in you. This process doesn't have to be formal, and in fact your advocates may not ever know that's how you view them.

Being forced to assemble a group of advisers rather than having one great boss can be an advantage. If you're too dependent on one person, you might fail to establish a resilient network and end up in the corporate abyss if your boss leaves the company. Further, while having your brand tied to one leader is an asset when that leader's stock is rising, if the leader falls out of favor, that closeness can create a reputational hit.

Prioritize Visibility

Without your boss putting you in front of stakeholders, you need to find your own platform. Look for cross-functional or internal projects that will involve or be debriefed to stakeholders. If one doesn't exist, propose a project that aligns with the corporate values or vision or that solves a stated need.

For example, a client of mine volunteered to start a diversity and inclusion working group to determine why the company wasn't attracting a diverse range of talent above the manager level, despite its being a stated corporate priority. She used her leadership and strategic skills to drive the process and presented the team's findings to the executive team. The CEO created a VP of diversity role and promoted her into it.

Find the Influencers and Offer to Help

In every organization there are centers of influence, some of which may not map to positional power. Think, for example, of the influence of a strategic adviser who retires from the executive team, or the CEO's long-standing assistant.

Babson College professor Rob Cross advises drawing maps of how people are connected in order to uncover spheres of influence in the organization, paying special attention to those with large numbers of connections. His research shows how new employees can succeed without a formal mentor by developing productive relationships with key opinion leaders.[2]

When you determine who the influencers are in your organization, make yourself helpful to them. Look at what you can offer them rather than just what they can give you. Contribute to their efforts without expecting a short-term return. Trust in the long-term benefit of the relationship. As Wharton professor Adam Grant notes in his book *Give and Take*, being a giver, as he calls it, is often far more beneficial and effective than being just a taker.

Use Positive Outside Pressure

Building your status outside the organization can often gain you visibility inside it. Corporate leaders notice who is visible to customers, stakeholders, and the broader industry. Professionals at any level can build a solid platform that has a greater reach than their position might indicate.

Choose a way to do this that is genuinely interesting to you. You might decide to join an industry association and work toward holding a leadership position there. You can build a following on social media by demonstrating expertise and engaging with known thinkers in your field. Corporate public relations departments are typically eager for employees to provide ideas and to be available for media interviews or article submissions. Ask members of the PR team how you can best assist them in their goals, and follow up on what they suggest. Bringing ideas around your interests and expertise—and continually feeding the PR team interesting topics—can make you a go-to resource.

Imagine a customer telling your leadership that one of the reasons they selected your company was because of an article you wrote about industry trends. This is not a far-fetched concept: I have heard clients include industry recognition as an important factor when evaluating team members. It's hard for even the best internal recognition to match external validation.

If you have the option, there's no question that finding a supportive boss with influence is a direct benefit to your career. But even that may not be enough. Companies are dynamic, and having other ways to advocate for yourself—or having others do it—is a more sustainable approach. Building a range of supporters who can help you grow in diverse ways may be the best advantage you can have.

Adapted from "How to Advance in Your Career When Your Boss Won't Help," on hbr.org, July 26, 2018 (product #H04G6I).

15

To Build Grit, Go Back to Basics

An interview with Shannon Huffman Polson
by Curt Nickisch

Concepts like resilience and grit have been popular in recent years. Shannon Huffman Polson knows all about the kind of mental and emotional fortitude that so many experts say people need—but few people actually have. She was one of the first women to pilot the Apache attack helicopter in the United States Army, has launched a successful corporate and consulting career, and is the author of *The Grit Factor: Courage, Resilience, and Leadership in the Most Male-Dominated Organization in the World*.

In this interview, she discusses how to develop grit and how it has helped her advocate for herself as a woman in an industry of mostly men.

CURT NICKISCH: *First and foremost, what does grit mean to you?*

SHANNON HUFFMAN POLSON: The way that I have defined it over the years is "*a dogged determination in the face of difficult circumstances.*" Angela Duckworth of the University of Pennsylvania has defined grit as "*passion and perseverance toward long-term goals,*" which I also love. I will say that in today's context—where the future is very uncertain, where the horizon is especially unclear, and where we're all working in these environments that are much more ambiguous—I have a slight preference for my own definition.

Tell me about that experience of facing obstacles as an aspiring pilot in the U.S. Army.

I certainly didn't go into it understanding the challenges. I went into the military, and into army attack aviation, because I wanted to do something hard and exciting. And I was 21 years old. I don't know what you know when you're 21, but fortunately not enough to dissuade you from what might lie ahead.

I approached it more with enthusiasm for the opportunity and the job. Of course, once I got into that position and saw the challenges I would face, especially as one of the first women in the role, it was a very different scenario than any that I had found myself in prior to that.

It had a lot less support and assurance than I had grown up with, for sure.

What did you encounter along the way?

When I was at Duke University, I was an English major and in the Army ROTC. The assumption was that I would then receive my commission in the National Guard going forward. At the end of my senior year, I drove out to Raleigh, North Carolina, to meet with the state aviation officer, where I would receive my assignment for the years ahead. I remember reporting to a colonel, who was probably in his late thirties. It seemed like he was behind this immense desk that was as wide as the room, with shiny windows going up the back. I stood at attention and saluted, and tried not to shake too much. He had me take a seat, and we exchanged a couple of pleasantries in a very formal sort of a way, before the exchange that I would never forget. He stopped midsentence, leaned back in his chair, looked down his nose at me, and said, "You realize, cadet, that you will never fly an attack aircraft."

I recognized his comment for what it was meant to be, which was small and mean, because at the time, in 1993, attack aircraft weren't open to women to fly. But I also understood in my extremely nascent military career that there are times when the only thing you can say is, "Yes, sir." So I said, "Yes, sir," and I went back to the Duke University ROTC detachment and requested a transfer out of the National Guard and onto active duty. Later that spring, Congress lifted the combat exclusion clause for aviation. Suddenly everything in the inventory was open to women and men to fly, and I reported to Fort Rucker later that year.

It is a moment where a lot of people would stop, right? Or accept the powers that be?

A big part of what begins the grit-forming process is deciding that you are going to be the person who is in charge of your own story. You are going to be the person that decides what your narrative will be. You can't choose the raw material, but you can decide how you're going to use it. Many people don't do that.

How do you take that first step?

It's really about focusing on that end goal and what your purpose is. When you're focused on that core purpose—that you are going to succeed, that you are going to contribute in this meaningful way—that allows you to not focus on the obstacles as much. It's a choice of where you put your focus.

Why is focusing on your own story so important?

The way that we understand information really is in the form of a story. Thinking back to make sense of our own stories—to understand the places where we grew, to understand our strengths, to understand where we overcame obstacles—becomes part of how we can approach future challenges or even current ones. It's thinking back and saying, "Hey, look at how I got through this really hard time. I either developed that strength or I realized there was a way around this." Doing that can help you find ways to negotiate the challenges that you're facing today, and that's critical work.

You aren't just making sense of the raw material that you're given. You're looking at how you turned the raw material of our life into your story. Because you get to choose. You get to say either, "I was a victim of this circumstance" or "I was able to overcome this. I was able to push through."

When you do that work, and you decide what that arc of that story of your life is going to be, then you can borrow from the strengths of that, understanding your values and how to go forward in connection with those values in a way that strengthens you for what you might be facing today or what you will be facing in the future.

You know your own story very well. How do you help people figure out what their story is, so that they know what to commit to?

There are a number of tactical exercises that I suggest. One of them is to start with what is sometimes called a journey line, or a lifeline. Look at your experiences, really own and understand the raw material of them, and get that down on paper. Then start to understand how that relates to and informs your core values and your core purpose.

There's another exercise that I love for drilling down into core purpose. This is pretty deep internal work; it's not back-of-the-napkin analysis. It requires time and space for you to think about—and to think about again and again. The exercise was developed by Toyota and is called the Five Whys. Ask yourself why you're doing something—not one time but five times. Drill down into that deep, deep why that's not specific to the job, that's not specific to the task, but that is truly connected to who you are as an individual. You've got to make that strong connection that is uniquely yours before you can apply it to whatever the task is, whatever the company is, whatever the company's missions and values and goals are. For me, it's service.

Was there a time in your military career where you faced obstacles, and recalling that core idea of service helped you get through them?

The best example I have for this is maybe one of the least exciting, but also one of the most relatable. When I first was assigned to Fort Bragg, North Carolina, that was my very first duty assignment, and I reported when I was 23 years old.

I was qualified in the Apache helicopter. I was excited. I was ready to fly and to lead. But when I arrived at Fort Bragg, in the 229th Aviation Regiment, there were two battalions. There were 120 male pilots, and I was the only female pilot. I was assigned not to a platoon where I would be flying and using the craft that I had just learned, but as the assistant to the assistant operations officer.

A desk job.

Exactly. And not just typing up, for example, operations orders where you're getting into the meat of things, but writing the appendices to the operations orders.

I was brought up believing that you do the best job you can, so I did the best job I could. I had great feedback, and I went to the captain I was working for and said, "Listen, sir. I'm going to keep doing the best job I can at this work, but I wonder when a platoon might open up." That captain looked at me and said, "Lieutenant, the army doesn't owe you anything."

I kept on doing my work, and then at some point we were all brought in on a Saturday to do work together as an operations shop for no apparent reason. The major that we all worked for looked over at me and joked, "Don't worry, Lieutenant, you'll be married by the time you're 25."

I did not say, "Yes, sir," as I had to that colonel back in Raleigh. But I went to see the major the next week, and

I said, "Sir, I'm going to keep doing the best job I can at what I've been assigned, but I think that I can do more." And he looked kind of surprised. Then he assigned me one additional duty after the other. And finally I took that first flight platoon.

But I think back on those times, and I think about the people and companies I have the chance to talk to across the country and around the world. I talk to people all the time who don't know how to push back when somebody says, "The army doesn't owe you anything," or "You'll be married by the time you're 25." They just think that's where they're stuck.

I really believe that there's an opportunity for us to push through those things by owning our story, by drilling down into core purpose, and by learning to have the courage to ask for what you want, and to ask again and again. Every single opportunity that I had in the military, I had to ask for. I had to earn it first, of course, and then I had to ask for it. And that's an important lesson in that whole process.

How do you start practicing grit? How do you start becoming better at it?

To get better at doing hard things, you need to do hard things. It sounds almost trite to say, but you take one step. You challenge yourself a little bit more the next time, and a little bit more the next time, and a little bit more the next time. That truly is how you build up what is essentially a muscle for grit and resilience. And it's something that is accessible to every single one of us.

Adapted from "To Build Grit, Go Back to Basics" on HBR IdeaCast *(podcast), September 1, 2020.*

SECTION FOUR

Support the Women Around You

16

Stop Telling Women They Have Impostor Syndrome

by Ruchika Tulshyan and Jodi-Ann Burey

Talisa Lavarry was exhausted. She had led the charge at her corporate event management company to plan a high-profile, security-intensive event, working around the clock and through weekends for months. Barack Obama was the keynote speaker.

Lavarry knew how to handle the complicated logistics required—but not the office politics. A golden opportunity to prove her expertise had turned into a living nightmare. Lavarry's colleagues interrogated and censured her, calling her professionalism into question. Their bullying, both subtle and overt, haunted each decision she made. Lavarry wondered whether her race had something to do with the way she was treated. She was, after all, the only Black woman on her team. She began doubting whether she was qualified for the job, despite constant praise from the client.

Things with her planning team became so acrimonious that Lavarry found herself demoted from lead to co-lead and eventually was unacknowledged altogether by her colleagues. Each action that chipped away at her role doubly chipped away at her confidence. She became plagued by deep anxiety, self-hatred, and the feeling that she was a fraud.

What had started as healthy nervousness—Will I fit in? Will my colleagues like me? Can I do good work?—became a workplace-induced trauma that had her contemplating suicide.

Today, when Lavarry reflects on the impostor syndrome she fell prey to during that time, she knows it wasn't a lack of self-confidence that held her back. It was repeatedly facing systemic racism and bias.

Examining Impostor Syndrome as We Know It

Impostor syndrome is loosely defined as doubting your abilities and feeling like a fraud. It disproportionately affects high-achieving people, who find it difficult to accept their accomplishments.[1]

Psychologists Pauline Rose Clance and Suzanne Imes developed the concept, originally termed impostor phenomenon, in their 1978 study, which focused on high-achieving women.[2] They posited that "despite outstanding academic and professional accomplishments, women who experience the impostor phenomenon persist in believing that they are really not bright and have fooled anyone who thinks otherwise." Their findings spurred decades of thought leadership, programs, and initiatives to address impostor syndrome in women. Even famous women—from Hollywood superstars such as Charlize Theron and Viola Davis to business leaders such as Sheryl Sandberg and even former First Lady Michelle Obama and Supreme Court Justice Sonia Sotomayor—have confessed to experiencing it. Common recommended solutions range from attending conferences to reading books to reciting one's accomplishments in front of a mirror. What's less explored is why impostor syndrome exists in the first place and what role workplace systems play in fostering and exacerbating it in women. We think there's room to question impostor syndrome as the reason women may be inclined to distrust their success.

The impact of systemic racism, classism, xenophobia, and other biases was categorically absent when the concept of impostor syndrome was first developed. Many groups were excluded from the study, namely women of color and people of various income levels, genders, and professional backgrounds. Even impostor syndrome as we know it today puts the blame on individuals, without accounting for the historical and cultural contexts that are foundational to how it manifests in both women of color and white women. Impostor syndrome directs our view toward fixing women at work instead of fixing the places where women work.

Feeling Unsure Shouldn't Make You an Impostor

Impostor syndrome took a fairly universal feeling of discomfort, second-guessing, and mild anxiety in the workplace and pathologized it, especially for women. As white men progress, their feelings of doubt usually abate as their work and intelligence are validated over time. They're able to find role models who are like them, and rarely (if ever) do others question their competence, contributions, or leadership style. Women experience the opposite. Rarely is there a women's career development conference where a session on overcoming impostor syndrome is not on the agenda.

The label of impostor syndrome is a heavy load to bear. "Impostor" brings a tinge of criminal fraudulence to the feeling of simply being unsure or anxious about joining a new team or learning a new skill. Add to that the medical undertone of "syndrome," which recalls the "female hysteria" diagnoses of the nineteenth century. Although feelings of uncertainty are an expected and normal part of professional life, women who experience them are deemed to *suffer* from impostor syndrome. Even if women demonstrate strength, ambition, and resilience, our daily battles with microaggressions, especially expectations and assumptions formed by stereotypes and racism, often push us down. Impostor syndrome as a concept fails to capture this dynamic and puts the onus on women to deal with the effects. Workplaces remain misdirected toward seeking individual solutions for issues disproportionately caused by systems of discrimination and abuses of power.

Bias and Exclusion Exacerbate Feelings of Doubt

For women of color, self-doubt and the feeling that we don't belong in corporate workplaces can be even more pronounced. Not because women of color (a broad, imprecise categorization) have an innate deficiency, but because the intersection of our race and gender often places us in a precarious position at work. Many of us across the world are implicitly, if not explicitly, told we don't belong in white- and male-dominated workplaces. According to a 2020 report from the Working Mother Research Institute, half of the women of color in the United States are thinking about leaving their jobs in the next two years, citing feelings of marginalization or disillusionment, which is consistent with our experiences.[3] Exclusion that exacerbated self-doubt was a key reason for each of our transitions from corporate workplaces to entrepreneurship.

"Who is deemed 'professional' is an assessment process that's culturally biased and skewed," says Tina Opie, an associate professor at Babson College. When employees from marginalized backgrounds try to hold themselves up to a standard that no one like them has met (and that they're often not expected to be able to meet), the pressure to excel can become too much to bear. The once-engaged Latina woman suddenly becomes quiet in meetings. The Indian woman who was a sure shot for promotion gets vague feedback about lacking leadership presence. The trans woman who always spoke up doesn't anymore because her manager makes gender-insensitive remarks. The Black woman whose questions helped create better products for the organization doesn't feel safe contributing feedback after being told she's not a team player. For women of color, universal feelings of doubt become magnified by chronic battles with systemic bias and racism.

In truth, we don't belong because we were never supposed to belong. Our presence in most of these spaces is a result of decades of grassroots activism and begrudgingly developed legislation. Academic institutions and corporations are still mired in the cultural inertia of old boys' clubs and white supremacy. Biased practices across institutions routinely stymie the ability of individuals from underrepresented groups to truly thrive.

The answer to overcoming impostor syndrome is not to fix individuals. It's to create an environment that fosters a variety of leadership styles and in which diverse racial, ethnic, and gender identities are seen as just as professional as the current model, which Opie describes as usually "Eurocentric, masculine, and heteronormative."

Confidence Doesn't Equal Competence

We often falsely equate confidence—most often the type demonstrated by white male leaders—with competence and leadership. Employees who can't (or won't) conform to male-biased social styles are told they have impostor syndrome. According to organizational psychologist Tomas Chamorro-Premuzic:

> *The truth of the matter is that pretty much anywhere in the world men tend to think that they are much smarter than women. Yet arrogance and overconfidence are inversely related to leadership talent—the ability to build and maintain high-performing teams, and to inspire followers to set aside their selfish agendas in order to work for the common interest of the group.*[4]

The same systems that reward confidence in male leaders, even if they're incompetent, punish white women for lacking confidence, women of color for showing too much of it, and all women for demonstrating it in a way that's deemed unacceptable. These biases are insidious and complex and stem from narrow definitions of acceptable behavior drawn from white male models of leadership. Research from Kecia M. Thomas, dean of the College of Arts and Sciences at the University of Alabama at Birmingham, finds that too often women of color enter their companies as "pets" but are treated as threats once they gain influence in their roles.[5] Women of color are by no means a monolith, but we are often linked by our common experiences of navigating stereotypes that hold us back from reaching our full potential.

Fixing Bias, Not Women

Impostor syndrome is especially prevalent in biased, toxic cultures that value individualism and overwork. Yet the "fix women's impostor syndrome" narrative has persisted, decade after decade. We see inclusive workplaces as a multivitamin that can ensure that women of color can thrive. Rather than focus on fixing impostor syndrome, professionals whose identities have been marginalized and discriminated against must experience a cultural shift writ large.

Leaders must create a culture for women and people of color that addresses systemic bias and racism. Only by doing so can we reduce the experiences that culminate in so-called impostor syndrome among employees from marginalized communities—or, at the very least, help those employees channel healthy self-doubt into positive motivation, which is best fostered within a supportive work culture.

Perhaps then we can stop misdiagnosing women with "impostor syndrome" once and for all.

Adapted from content posted on hbr.org, February 11, 2021 (product #H066HL).

17

How Gender Bias Corrupts Performance Reviews

by Paola Cecchi-Dimeglio

The annual performance review already has many strikes against it. Harried managers end up recalling high and low points on the fly; employees often get unclear direction.

Here's another flaw: Women are shortchanged by these reviews. In my forthcoming book on race and gender bias in the workplace, *Diversity Dividend*, I present scores of successful interventions I have used in large domestic and international professional services firms to level the playing field for women in appraisals and promotions, among other areas. One of my findings, using content analysis of individual annual performance reviews, shows that women were 1.4 times more likely to receive critical subjective feedback than either positive feedback or critical objective feedback.

That's because annual evaluations *are* often subjective, which opens the door to issues including gender bias ("Tom is more comfortable and independent than Carolyn in handling the client's concerns") and confirmation bias ("I knew she'd struggle with that project").

I found that these biases can lead to double standards, in that a situation can get a positive or a negative spin, depending on gender. In one review I read, the manager noted, "Heidi seems to shrink when she's around others, and especially around clients; she needs to be more self-confident." But a similar problem—confidence in working with clients—was given a positive spin when a man was struggling with it: "Jim needs to develop his natural ability to work with people."

In another pair of reviews, the reviewer highlighted the woman's "analysis paralysis," while the same behavior in a male colleague was seen as careful thoughtfulness: "Simone seems paralyzed and confused when facing tight deadlines to make decisions," while "Cameron seems hesitant in making decisions, yet he is able to work out multiple alternative solutions and determine the most suitable one." Double standards like these clearly affect women's opportunities for advancement.

It does your company no good when employees are overrated because of subjective biases, including leniency (for example, an employee dropped the ball, but "he had a lot on his plate") and the "halo effect," where one positive trait is assumed to be linked to others ("He inspires confidence, which goes a long way").

My data also revealed that women got less constructively critical feedback. The objective of constructive feedback is to allow an employee to focus on the positives while identifying areas where there is room for growth. For example, such feedback might be, "Stephanie, your replies to partners about client matters are often not on point" rather than "Stephanie, you have missed important opportunities to provide clear and concise information, such as X. I have some thoughts on how you could prevent that from happening again, such as Y." These findings are in line with research from my colleagues at Stanford University, Shelley Correll and Caroline Simard, whose work suggests that women receive vaguer feedback than men do.[1]

Finally, women's performance was more likely to be attributed to characteristics such as luck or their ability to spend long hours in the office, which was perceived as real commitment to the firm, rather than their abilities and skills. As such, they often did not receive due credit for their work.

The good news is that the performance appraisal system can be fixed. By using more-objective criteria, involving a broader group of reviewers, and adjusting the frequency of reviews, it is possible to remove subjective biases that creep in.

Specifically, my field experiments at professional services firms suggest that the use of tailor-made, automated, real-time communication tools with instant feedback on employees' weekly performance from supervisors, colleagues, and clients can have dramatic results for women.

As opposed to the traditional annual feedback system, these instruments were designed to remove bias from answers (for example, the language of the feedback options is gender-neutral) and help the reviewers to provide constructive feedback. The order of requested feedback was given careful consideration in the instruments' design, all in an effort to create a level playing field.

Another benefit is that having more-frequent feedback gives opportunities to recognize different styles of leadership. As the seminal work of social psychologist Alice Eagly has demonstrated, there are gender differences in leadership styles.[2] Her work, followed by that of other researchers, has revealed that women's leadership styles are less hierarchical and more cooperative, participatory, and collaborative than their male counterparts'.[3]

Women's strengths, such as their collaborative and participatory styles, were more easily recognized when using this new appraisal system. For example, instant feedback included: "The employee is a team player and understands how to help others in time of need" or "The employee contributes to the success of the team on a regular basis." In other words, it resulted in the information used for developmental and assessment purposes being more accurate and gender-neutral.

Giving frequent feedback might sound like a lot of work, especially for large teams. It's not. Feedback involves two to six reviewers per week, and takes each of them no more than 15 minutes.

One of the other benefits is that the clients who participated in these experiments were asked to evaluate the performance of the people who served them. The clients felt listened to and engaged in the process of providing constructive feedback on what they valued in the relationship and how they could be better served.

For example, colleagues might rate each other on the criterion that "clear information is provided to the client during the call," while clients are asked whether the employee serving them "addressed my concerns and showed interest during the call." These evaluations are collected over time in a broader category called "client relationship."

The responses are weighted by how much exposure the feedback providers have to the person they are rating. On a quarterly basis, the employee sits down with the manager for a check-in and goes over the results.

The advantages of this approach, compared with annual reviews, are myriad for managers:

- They receive objective criteria to provide a comprehensive look at performance. Moreover, they get detail they've never had before: how constant employees' performance is, how they grow over the course of the year (or the project cycle), how they respond to feedback over time, what their weak and strong points are, and which areas they excel in.

- They can observe the employee and value the person's behavior in different contexts, as each reviewer provides input and expresses preferences for certain styles. Managers can see how various appraisers attach different weights to the same aspects of performance they experienced.
- In turn, managers learn the kind of support and exposure they need to provide each employee for optimal performance with supervisors, peers, subordinates, and clients.

Employees being reviewed gain as well:

- They're evaluated for their actual performance and work relationships, not by their boss's impressions. In my research, the likelihood of women receiving subjective feedback in the form of negative personality-based criticism disappears or significantly decreases with this approach.
- They get a diagnostic instrument that facilitates self-management, because real-time reviews give

examples of effective (or ineffective) behavior and convey information on what the individual must start, stop, or continue doing.

Companies can start leveling the playing field by redesigning their performance appraisal system with a few simple steps:

- Invest in systems that crowdsource and continually collect data about the performance of people and teams. Crowdsourcing performance data throughout the year yields even better insights about your staff.
- Train appraisers to give feedback about specific criteria that the employer and employee agree to. The resulting appraisal of the person on these criteria is then perceived as fairer.
- Develop an appraisal scale that specifies what an employee must start doing, stop doing, or continue doing by tenure and project cycle.
- Transform what feedback is meant to achieve, using a tool with gender-neutral criteria.

Adapted from "How Gender Bias Corrupts Performance Reviews, and What to Do About It," on hbr.org, April 12, 2017 (product #H03LIY).

18

What Men Can Do to Be Better Advocates for Women

by Rania H. Anderson and David G. Smith

Advocating for women's advancement at work is integral for improving financial results, gender balance, and diversity in our workplaces and leadership teams. Yet data from the Working Mother Research Institute finds that, while 48% of men say they have received detailed information on career paths to jobs with profit-and-loss responsibility in the past 24 months, just 15% of women report the same. And while 54% of men had a career discussion with a mentor or sponsor in the past 24 months, only 39% of women did.[1]

Why? Because leaders, the majority of whom are male and white, don't adequately sponsor or mentor people who don't look like them. Research from Coqual (formerly the Center for Talent Innovation) found that a full 71% of executives have protégés whose gender or race match their own.[2] That means that women and minorities don't benefit from sponsorship like their male colleagues do, and organizations lose out by not drawing on the full potential of their talent.

Confusion about the #MeToo movement may have unintentionally exacerbated the situation. Two 2018 surveys by Lean In and Bloomberg Media found that, in the wake of high-profile workplace sexual harassment and assault allegations, some men began to *avoid* professional work relationships with women.[3] It was even a topic at a World Economic Forum event: Senior male executives talked about avoiding one-on-one mentoring relationships as a risk management strategy.

This response is not productive. There are plenty of men who want to do what's best for their businesses and employees. We find that sponsorship and advocacy make the biggest difference.

Sponsors, by definition, use their position and power to achieve business objectives by advancing a protégé's career. They are not benevolent benefactors. They are influential leaders who intentionally invest in, and rely on, the skills and contributions of their protégés to achieve their own goals and their protégé's highest potential. A sponsor needs to know the skills and capabilities of their protégés, see their potential, and be able to orchestrate their advancement—but they don't have to show them how to play the instrument or encourage them to practice.

And while mentors may or may not have the same level of power as sponsors, they frequently have a great deal more influence than they actually use. We regularly see mentors support their mentees privately but be reluctant to advocate for them.

If companies truly want to improve their financial results and diversity, they need to do a better job of developing sponsors for women and people of color at all levels of their organization. Leaders are regularly taught about strategic thinking, championing change, making financial decisions, and managing people, but they are not taught how to become sponsors or maximize their impact in the role. As a result, white men don't have the skills to advance women and people of color—even though they unconsciously help other white men to do so. Rather than be frustrated by or blame male leaders, companies need to better enlist and equip them to excel. And men need to consistently implement what they learn.

All of this starts with understanding what the best sponsors do and how they do it. Here are the seven key steps we've identified based on our experiences advising global leaders and companies.

Identify high-potential talent

Great sponsors purposefully look for people who bring different experiences and perspectives from their own and have the results, potential, and ambition to make a larger contribution. If they can't identify someone on their own, they go out of their way to ask HR and other leaders to recommend candidates.

Stan, an executive director of a regional bank and a coaching client of one of us (Rania), is a great example of this type of sponsor. He recognized the potential in one of his employees, Beth. Even though she had no prior financial services experience when she joined the bank, she was great at developing client, community, and internal relationships, and Stan could see that, if she held a senior leadership role, she could make a broader contribution. He decided to sponsor her to fast-track her into a senior market role.

Determine the best stretch role

It is vital to identify high-visibility opportunities that could benefit from your protégé's perspectives, talents, and experiences—and in which they can excel. These should be roles or projects that, if executed successfully, will clearly benefit the business as well their career. The best opportunities to develop protégés are those that involve some of these conditions: profit and loss, high risk, strategic clients, strategic importance to the business, starting something new, or fixing a business problem. Stan did this by recognizing that Beth's management skills would make a notable improvement in their market's retail division.

Similarly, when Jay, an executive at a fast-growth financial services startup, recognized that his employee Lexi had the talent to achieve more significant results and advance, he assigned her several complex business challenges that required her to interact with senior leaders across the organization. After she successfully addressed them, she gained positive visibility.

Position the role

Stretch assignments can be challenging, so great mentors ensure their protégés understand that the organization values and thinks highly of them. Many women want and appreciate this type of encouragement and may be hesitant to take a challenging role without it.[4] Protégés should be provided with context on the importance of new opportunities, what a sponsor believes they can accomplish, and how the sponsor and the company will support them. Have their manager and mentors encourage them to persist in spite of the obstacles they will inevitably encounter. In Stan's case, he talked to Beth about why he thought she'd excel in leading the retail banking group and what success in that role could mean for her in the future.

Provide opportunities for development and support

Sponsors must ensure that people in their organization invest time, expertise, resources, and budget to help give protégés the skills and experiences they need to be successful. This is where mentors and other advisers come in. As Beth demonstrated results, Stan arranged for her to have technical skill and leadership development experiences. Both Beth and Lexi were provided with executive leadership coaching.

It's also important to educate leaders who will work with a protégé about the challenges women, people of color, and especially women of color often encounter in the workplace. (See chapter 13.) It's also worth exploring if a protégé can be connected with people in similar life and career stages or those who have had success navigating through personal and professional challenges.

Pave the way

Sponsors have a responsibility to introduce their protégés to influential and powerful people in their organization or industry, including clients, especially if they are crucial for success in their work. In Lexi's case, this meant having her travel internationally to meet with key partners and assigning her an important leadership role on a transition team. She delivered stellar results. In both Beth's and Lexi's cases, their sponsor regularly communicated their results and advocated for them with other senior executives.

Help protégés persist

No matter the stretch assignment, there will always be challenges and setbacks. Sponsors must make sure criticism, mistakes, failures, or naysayers don't derail their protégés. That doesn't mean sheltering them from adversity; it does mean ensuring that the organization is understanding and patient if everything doesn't work out the first time. More often than not, success takes more than one assignment.

Champion promotions and recognition

Sponsors advocate for raises, promotions, and recognition to deserving protégés. As Beth delivered, Stan gave her additional responsibilities that have prepared her for a significant promotion. Lexi later advanced into a senior leadership role. It took her excellent performance, advocating for herself, and Jay's advocacy to the rest of his executive committee teammates to make that happen.

Our experience and the data show that women receive less sponsorship and advocacy in mentorship than their male colleagues. This imbalance is one of the primary reasons they don't advance at the same pace as men and leave their places of employment.[5]

Leaders who take these steps will become better, more inclusive sponsors, which will improve their own results, the careers of protégés, and the organizations where they work. According to a number of studies, gender balance in companies and on teams improves a host of outcomes including financial results, innovation, decision making, organizational commitment, retention, and job satisfaction. And managers who identify and develop all high-potential talent are more successful and are recognized for this approach.

Companies can encourage this kind of sponsorship by clearly defining the steps, behaviors, and expectations for people in formal programs. They can deliberately address the mandate and process for the advocacy and sponsorship of women and people of color in their employee development programs and performance assessments. And finally, they can hold senior managers accountable for sponsorship. It is not only good for women and people of color; it's also good for the business and the sponsors.

Adapted from "What Men Can Do to Be Better Mentors and Sponsors to Women," on hbr.org, August 7, 2019 (product #H0525R).

19

The Power of Women Supporting Women

by Anne Welsh McNulty

As my experience of advancing from rookie accountant to managing director at an investment bank taught me, conversations between women have massive benefits for the individual and the organization. When I graduated college in the 1970s, I believed that women would quickly achieve parity at all levels of professional life now that we had "arrived"—I viewed the lack of women at the top as a pipeline problem, not a cultural one. But my expectation of finding support from female colleagues—the feeling of sisterhood in this mission—didn't survive first contact with the workplace.

When I was a first-year accountant at a Big Eight firm (now there's only the Big Four), I kept asking the only woman senior to me to go to lunch, until finally she told me, "Look, there's only room for one female partner here.

You and I are not going to be friends." Unfortunately, she was acting rationally. Senior-level women who champion younger women are more likely to get negative performance reviews, according to a 2016 study in the *Academy of Management Journal*.[1]

My brusque colleague's behavior has a (misogynistic) academic name: the "queen bee" phenomenon. Some senior-level women distance themselves from junior women, perhaps to be more accepted by their male peers. As a study published in the *Leadership Quarterly* concludes, this is a *response* to inequality at the top, not the cause.[2] Trying to separate oneself from a marginalized group is, sadly, a strategy that's frequently employed. It's easy to believe that there's limited space for people who look like you when you can see it with your own eyes.

By contrast, men are 46% more likely to have a higher-ranking advocate in the office, according to economist Sylvia Ann Hewlett.[3] This makes an increasing difference in representation as you go up the org chart. According to a 2016 McKinsey report, white men hold 36% of entry-level corporate jobs and white women hold 31%.[4] But at the very first rung above that, those numbers are 47% for white men and 26% for white women—a 16% drop. For women of color, the drop from 17% to 11% is a plunge of 35%. People tend to think that whatever conditions exist now are "normal." Maybe this (charitably) explains men's blind spots: At companies where only one in ten senior leaders are women, says McKinsey, nearly 50% of men felt women were "well represented" in leadership.

Worse than being snubbed by the woman above me was the lack of communication between women at my level. Of the fifty auditors in my class, five were women. All of us were on different client teams. At the end of my first year, I was shocked and surprised to learn that all four of the other women had quit or been fired—shocked at the outcome, and surprised because we hadn't talked among ourselves enough to understand what was happening. During that year, I'd had difficult experiences with men criticizing me, commenting on my looks, or flatly saying I didn't deserve to work there—but I had no idea that the other women were having similar challenges. We expected our performance to be judged as objectively as our clients' books, and we didn't realize the need to band together until it was too late. Each of us had dealt with those challenges individually, and obviously not all successfully.

I resolved not to let either of those scenarios happen again; I wanted to be aware of what was going on with the women I worked with. As I advanced in my career, I hosted women-only lunches and created open channels of communication. I made it a point to reach out to each woman who joined the firm with an open-door policy, sharing advice and my personal experiences, including how to say no to doing traditionally gendered (and uncompensated) tasks like getting coffee or taking care of the office environment. To personal assistants, who might find some of those tasks unavoidable, I emphasized that they could talk to me about any issues in the workplace, that their roles were critical, and that they should be treated with respect. The lunches were essential, providing a dedicated space to share challenges and successes. Coming together as a group made people realize that their problems weren't specific to them, but in fact were collective obstacles. All of this vastly improved the flow of information and relieved tension and anxiety. It reassured us that although our jobs were challenging, we were not alone. In doing so, I hope it lowered the attrition rate of women working at my company; across all corporate jobs, attrition is stubbornly higher for women than for men, especially women of color.[5]

My own daughter has arrived at a workplace that has not changed nearly as much as I had hoped—although 40% of Big Four accounting firm employees are women, they make up only 19% of audit partners.[6] Only one in five C-suite members are women, and they are still less likely than their male peers to report that there are equal opportunities for advancement.[7]

What are women in the workplace to do when research shows that we're penalized for trying to lift each other up? The antidote to being penalized for sponsoring women may just be to do it more—and to do it vocally, loudly, and proudly—until we're able to change perceptions. There are massive benefits for the individual and the organization when women support each other. The advantages of sponsorship for protégés may be clear, such as getting access to opportunities and having their achievements brought to the attention of senior management, but sponsors gain as well, by becoming known as cultivators of talent and as leaders. Importantly, organizations that welcome such sponsorship benefit too—creating a supportive culture where talent is recognized and rewarded for all employees. Sponsorship is also an excellent way for men to be allies at work.

But there's still so much work that needs to be done. I'm thrilled by the rise of women's organizations like Sallie Krawcheck's Ellevate Network, a professional network of women supporting each other across companies to change the culture of business at large. (I'm especially fond of it because it began as "85 Broads," a network of Goldman Sachs alumnae that drew its name from the old GS headquarters address before Krawcheck, a Merrill Lynch alumna, bought and expanded it.) That network spawned a sibling, Ellevest, an investment firm focused on women and companies that advance women. Other ventures include Dee Poku-Spalding's WIE Network (Women Inspiration and Enterprise), a leadership network whose mission is to support women in their career ambitions by providing real-world learning via access to established business leaders. I am attempting to make my own dent in this area, having endowed the Anne Welsh McNulty Institute for Women's Leadership at my alma mater, Villanova University, to support new research and leadership development opportunities for women.

These are wonderful supplements, but they can't replace the benefits of and the necessity for connections among women inside a company—at and across all levels. It reduces the feeling of competition for an imaginary quota at the top. It helps other women realize, "Oh, it's not just me"—a revelation that can change the course of a woman's career. It's also an indispensable way of identifying bad actors and systemic problems within the company. It need not be a massive program, and you don't need to overthink it—in fact, there's a healthy debate about affinity groups run from the top down. Whether you are a first-year employee or a manager, just reach out and make those connections. I'm guessing you'll find that the return on investment on the cost of a group lunch will be staggering.

Adapted from "Don't Underestimate the Power of Women Supporting Each Other at Work," on hbr.org, September 3, 2018 (product #H04HSC).

NOTES

Chapter 2

1. Madeline E Heilman and Tyler G Okimoto, "Why Are Women Penalized for Success at Male Tasks?: The Implied Communality Deficit," *Journal of Applied Psychology* 92, no. 1 (2007): 81–92; Amy J. C. Cuddy, Susan T. Fiske, and Peter Glick, "When Professionals Become Mothers, Warmth Doesn't Cut the Ice," *Journal of Social Issues* 60 (2004): 701–718.

2. Wei Zheng, Olca Surgevil, and Ronit Kark, "Dancing on the Razor's Edge: How Top-Level Women Leaders Manage the Paradoxical Tensions Between Agency and Communion," *Sex Roles* 79 (2018): 633–650.

Chapter 3

1. Shonda Rhimes, "My Year of Saying Yes to Everything," filmed February 2016. TED video. https://www.ted.com/talks/shonda_rhimes_my_year_of_saying_yes_to_everything?language=en.

2. Lakshmi Ramarajan and Erin Reid, "Shattering the Myth of Separate Worlds: Negotiating Nonwork Identities at Work," *Academy of Management Review* 38 (2013): 621–644.

3. "Meghan Markle: I'm More Than an 'Other,'" *Elle*, December 22, 2016, https://www.elle.com/uk/life-and-culture/news/a26855/more-than-an-other.

4. Lakshmi Ramarajan, Nancy P. Rothbard, and Steffanie L. Wilk, "Discordant vs. Harmonious Selves: The Effects of Identity Conflict and Enhancement on Sales Performance in Employee–Customer Interactions," *Academy of Management Review* 60 (2017): 2208–2238; Niklas K. Steffens et al., "How Multiple Social Identities Are Related to Creativity," *Personality and Social Psychology Bulletin* 42, no. 2 (2016): 188–203.

5. Brianna Barker Caza, Sherry Moss, and Heather Vough, "From Synchronizing to Harmonizing: The Process of Authenticating Multiple Work Identities," *Administrative Science Quarterly* 63 no. 4 (December 2018): 703–745. https://doi.org/10.1177/0001839217733972.

6. Andrew Molinsky, "Cross-Cultural Code-Switching: The Psychological Challenges of Adapting Behavior in Foreign Cultural Interactions," *Academy of Management* 32, no. 2 (April 2007).

Chapter 4

1. Bernard M. Bass and Francis J. Yammarino, "Congruence of Self and Others' Leadership Ratings of Naval Officers for Understanding Successful Performance," *Applied Psychology* 40, no. 4 (1991): 437–454; Paul J. Silvia and Maureen E. O'Brien, "Self-Awareness and Constructive Functioning: Revisiting 'the Human Dilemma,'" *Journal of Social and Clinical Psychology* 23, no. 4 (2004): 475–489; Kenneth N. Wexley et al., "Attitudinal Congruence and Similarity as Related to Interpersonal Evaluations in Manager–Subordinate Dyads," *Academy of Management Journal* 23, no. 2 (1980): 320–330.

2. Ellen Van Velsor, Sylvester Taylor, and Jean B. Leslie, "An Examination of the Relationships Among Self-Perception Accuracy, Self-Awareness, Gender, and Leader Effectiveness," *Human Resource Management* 32, no. 2–3 (1993): 249–263; Scott Taylor and Jacqueline Hood, "It May Not Be What You Think: Gender Differences in Predicting Emotional and Social Competence," *Human Relations* 64, no. 5 (2011): 627–652.

3. Pedja Stevanovic and Patricia Rupert, "Career-Sustaining Behaviors, Satisfactions, and Stresses of Professional Psychologists," *Psychotherapy: Theory, Research, Practice, Training* 41, no. 3 (2004): 301–309.

4. Judith L. Meece et al., "Sex Differences in Math Achievement: Toward a Model of Academic Choice," *Psychological Bulletin* 91, no. 2 (1982): 324–348; Kristen C. Kling et al., "Gender Differences in Self-Esteem: A Meta-Analysis," *Psychological Bulletin* 125, no. 4 (1999): 470–500.

5. Arthur I. Wohlers and Manuel London, "Ratings of Managerial Characteristics: Evaluation Difficulty, Co-worker Agreement, and Self-Awareness," *Personnel Psychology* 42, no. 2 (1989): 235–261; Rachel E. Sturm et al., "Leader Self-Awareness: An Examination and Implications of Women's Under-Prediction," *Journal of Organizational Behavior* 35, no. 5 (2014): 657–677.

6. Taylor and Hood. "It May Not Be What You Think."

7. Sturm et al., "Leader Self-Awareness."; Crystal L. Hoyt and Jeni L. Burnette, "Gender Bias in Leader Evaluations: Merging Implicit Theories and Role Congruity Perspectives," *Personality and Social Psychology Bulletin* 39, no. 10 (2013): 1306–1319; Lori A. Beaman et al., "Powerful Women: Does Exposure Reduce Bias?," working paper 14198, National Bureau of Economic Research, Cambridge, 2008, https://www.nber.org/system/files/working_papers/w14198/w14198.pdf.

8. Lareina Yee et al., *Women in the Workplace 2016* (McKinsey & Company and Lean In, 2016).

9. Shelley J. Correll and Caroline Simard, "Research: Vague Feedback Is Holding Women Back," hbr.org, April 29, 2016, https://hbr.org/2016/04/research-vague-feedback-is-holding-women-back.

10. Lori Nishiura Mackenzie, JoAnne Wehner, and Shelley J. Correll, "Why Most Performance Evaluations Are Biased, and How to Fix Them," hbr.org, January 11, 2019, https://hbr.org/2019/01/why-most-performance-evaluations-are-biased-and-how-to-fix-them.

11. Sturm et al., "Leader Self-Awareness."

12. Tomi-Ann Roberts, "Gender and the Influences of Evaluation on Self-Assessment in Achievement Settings," *Psychological Bulletin* 109, no. 2 (1991): 297–308.

13. Simine Vazire and Erika Carlson, "Others Sometimes Know Us Better Than We Know Ourselves," *Current Directions in Psychological Science* 20, no. 2 (2011): 104–108; Bass and Yammarino, "Congruence of Self.".

Chapter 13

1. "Infographic: The Women's & Multicultural Market Opportunity," Prudential, accessed July 20, 2021, http://www.prudential.com/media/managed/totalmarket/tm-infographic-women-multicultural-market-opportunity.html; *The 2017 State of Women-Owned Businesses Report* (American Express, 2017), https://ventureneer.com/wp-content/uploads/2017/11/2017-AMEX-SWOB-FINAL.pdf.

2. Vivian Hunt et al., *Delivering Through Diversity* (McKinsey & Company, 2018), https://www.mckinsey.com/~/media/mckinsey/business%20functions/organization/our%20insights/delivering%20through%20diversity/delivering-through-diversity_full-report.ashx.

3. Paul Gompers and Silpa Kovvali, "The Other Diversity Dividend," *Harvard Business Review*, July–August 2018, https://hbr.org/2018/07/the-other-diversity-dividend.

4. Georges Desvaux et al., *Women Matter: Time to Accelerate—Ten Years of Insights into Gender Diversity* (McKinsey & Company, 2017), https://www.mckinsey.com/~/media/mckinsey/featured%20insights/women%20matter/women%20matter%20ten%20years%20of%20insights%20on%20the%20importance%20of%20gender%20diversity/women-matter-time-to-accelerate-ten-years-of-insights-into-gender-diversity.pdf.

5. Cindy Ruth Pace, "Exploring Leadership Aspirations and Learning of Diverse Women Progressing Toward Top Leadership" (PhD diss., Columbia University, 2017), https://www.proquest.com/openview/d2671c00065fd641b5d7f59eebf5d2f3/1?pq-origsite=gscholar&cbl=18750&diss=y.

6. Dnika J. Travis and Jennifer Thorpe-Moscon, *Day-to-Day Experiences of Emotional Tax Among Women and Men of Color in the Workplace* (Catalyst, 2018), https://www.catalyst.org/research/day-to-day-experiences-of-emotional-tax-among-women-and-men-of-color-in-the-workplace.

7. Sylvia Ann Hewlett et al., *Vaulting the Color Bar: How Sponsorship Levers Multicultural Professionals into Leadership* (Center for Talent Innovation, 2012), https://www.talentinnovation.org/_private/assets/VaultingTheColorBar-KeyFindings-CTI.pdf.

8. Joan C. Williams and Marina Multhaup, "For Women and Minorities to Get Ahead, Managers Must Assign Work Fairly," hbr.org, March 5, 2018, https://hbr.org/2018/03/for-women-and-minorities-to-get-ahead-managers-must-assign-work-fairly.

Chapter 14

1. Sarah Green Carmichael, "Asking for Advice Makes People Think You're Smarter," June 2, 2016, in *HBR IdeaCast*, podcast, https://hbr.org/podcast/2016/06/asking-for-advice-makes-people-think-youre-smarter.html.

2. Rob Cross and Peter Gray, "The Best Way to Network in a New Job," hbr.org, March 19, 2018, https://hbr.org/2018/03/the-best-way-to-network-in-a-new-job.

Chapter 16

1. Kirsten Weir, "Feel Like a Fraud?" *gradPSYCH* 11, no. 4 (2013): 24.

2. Pauline Rose Clance and Suzanne Imes, "The Impostor Phenomenon in High Achieving Women: Dynamics and Therapeutic Intervention," *Psychotherapy Theory, Research and Practice* 15, no. 3 (1978): 241–247.

3. Barbara Frankel, "Half of Multicultural Women Are Thinking of Quitting. Here's Why," Working Mother, May 27, 2020, https://www.workingmother.com/why-women-of-color-want-to-quit.

4. Tomas Chamorro-Premuzic, "Why Do So Many Incompetent Men Become Leaders?" hbr.org, August 22, 2013, https://hbr.org/2013/08/why-do-so-many-incompetent-men.

5. Kecia Thomas, "Social Psychology Research on Women of Color in the STEM Disciplines." Presented at the Gender Summit, Washington DC, November 14, 2013. https://gender-summit.com/images/GS3NA_ppts/Thomas.pdf

Chapter 17

1. Shelley J. Correll and Caroline Simard, "Research: Vague Feedback Is Holding Women Back," hbr.org, April 29, 2016, https://hbr.org/2016/04/research-vague-feedback-is-holding-women-back.

2. Alice Eagly and Linda L. Carli, "Women and the Labyrinth of Leadership," *Harvard Business Review*, September 2007.

3. Herminia Ibarra and Otilia Obodaru, "Women and the Vision Thing," *Harvard Business Review*, January 2009.

Chapter 18

1. Barbara Frankel, Suzanne Richards, and Maria Ferris, *The Gender Gap at the Top* (Working Mother Research Institute, 2019), https://www.workingmother.com/sites/workingmother.com/files/attachments/2019/06/women_at_the_top_correct_size.pdf.

2. *The Sponsor Dividend* (Coqual, 2019), https://coqual.org/reports/the-sponsor-dividend.

3. "Working Relationships in the #MeToo Era: Key Findings," Lean In, 2019, https://leanin.org/sexual-harassment-backlash-survey-results; Gillian Tan and Katia Porzecanski, "Wall Street Rule for the #MeToo Era: Avoid Women at All Cost," Bloomberg, December 3, 2018, https://www.bloomberg.com/news/articles/2018-12-03/a-wall-street-rule-for-the-metoo-era-avoid-women-at-all-cost.

4. Raina Brands and Isabel Fernandez-Mateo, "Women Are Less Likely to Apply for Executive Roles If They've Been Rejected Before," hbr.org, February 7, 2017, https://hbr.org/2017/02/women-are-less-likely-to-apply-for-executive-roles-if-theyve-been-rejected-before.

5. Herminia Ibarra, Nancy M. Carter, and Christine Silva, "Why Men Still Get More Promotions Than Women," *Harvard Business Review*, September 2010.

Chapter 19

1. David R. Hekman, Stefanie K. Johnson, Maw-Der Foo and Wei Yang, "Does Diversity-Valuing Behavior Result in Diminished Performance Ratings for Non-White and Female Leaders?" *Academy of Management Journal* 60, no. 2 (2016).

2. Belle Derks, Colette Van Laar, and Naomi Ellemers, "The Queen Bee Phenomenon: Why Women Leaders Distance Themselves from Junior Women," *The Leadership Quarterly* 27, no. 3 (2016): 456–469.

3. Jessica Bennett, "Do Women-Only Networking Groups Help or Hurt Female Entrepreneurs?" *Inc.* Magazine (October 2017), https://www.inc.com/magazine/201710/jessica-bennett/women-coworking-spaces.html.

4. Alexis Krivkovich et al., *Women in the Workplace 2017* (McKinsey & Company, 2017), https://www.mckinsey.com/~/media/McKinsey/Industries/Technology%20Media%20and%20Telecommunications/High%20Tech/Our%20Insights/Women%20in%20the%20Workplace%202017/Women-in-the-Workplace-2017-v2.ashx.

5. Ibid.

6. Terry Sheridan, "Women Audit Partners Are Few and Far Between, Study Finds," AccountingWEB, July 24, 2017, https://www.accountingweb.com/practice/team/women-audit-partners-are-few-and-far-between-study-finds.

7. Krivkovich et al., "Women in the Workplace 2017."

INDEX

Discussion Guide

Since the *Women at Work* podcast first launched, we've heard from all over the world that it has inspired discussions and listening groups. We hope that this book does the same—that you'll want to share what you've learned with others. The questions in this discussion guide will help you talk about the challenges women face in the workplace and how we can work together to overcome them.

You don't need to have read the book from start to finish to participate. To get the most out of your discussion, think about the size of your group. A big group has the advantage of spreading ideas more widely—whether throughout your organization or among your friends and peers—but might lose some of the honesty and connection a small group would have. You may want to assign someone to lead the discussion to ensure that all participants are included, especially if some attendees are joining virtually. And it's a good idea to establish ground rules around privacy and confidentiality. *Women at Work* topics touch on difficult issues surrounding sexism and racism, so consider using trigger warnings.

Finally, think about what you want to accomplish in your discussion. Do you want to create a network of mutual support? Hope to disrupt the status quo? Or are you simply looking for an empathetic ear? With your goals in mind, use the questions that follow to advance the conversation about women at work.

1. What leadership traits are valued in your organization? Do you feel these are a fair representation of what both men *and* women can bring to the table? What are some of the double binds you've faced as you've pursued promotions and leadership positions?

2. In chapter 1, Nicole asks Tina Opie what the difference is between being inauthentic and being pushed out of your comfort zone. As you think about becoming a leader, how would you answer this question?

3. Think back to an instance where you were angry or frustrated at work. How did you respond? Did your reaction help or hurt the situation, and what would you do differently next time? How are strong emotions generally handled in your workplace?

4. In chapter 5, Muriel Maignan Wilkins and Amy Jen Su describe the first time they were seen as leaders. Have you had a moment when you were first seen as a leader—formally or informally? Who saw you as that leader, and what did they say or do that conveyed that feeling to you?

5. What are the largest struggles you've faced as you work to embody leadership presence and develop

your leadership voice? How have others responded to you?

6. What are the qualities you want in a sponsor? If you have a sponsor, how did you ask the person to take on that role, and what are some ways that you work together productively? If you don't have a sponsor, what are some of the barriers you're facing in securing this relationship?

7. In chapter 10, Amy Jen Su says we need to stop thinking that claiming credit is the same as bragging or self-promotion—something to feel "icky" about—and start seeing it as taking ownership of our work. How have you advocated for yourself in the past? Has someone ever stolen credit for your work? How did you respond? What would you do differently now?

8. Describe a time when you discussed promotion and growth opportunities with your boss. Was your boss supportive? What worked in that conversation—and what didn't?

9. In chapter 13, Cindy Pace describes the difficult path for women of color as they aspire to leadership positions. If you're a woman of color, did you relate to what she says, and have you tried any of these tactics? If you're not a woman of color, what have you observed in your own organization with regard to intersectionality and leadership?

10. In chapter 15, Shannon Huffman Polson shares some harsh statements that her army superiors said to her—that the army doesn't owe her anything and she'll be married by the time she's 25. Have you heard similar comments in your own career? How have you rebounded from such statements and attitudes?
11. What does the leadership team at the top of your organization look like? Is there diversity reflected in the group? Do you see opportunities for you to grow into leadership there, based on what you see?
12. Are the ways that promotion and leadership decisions are made in your organization fair? Where do you see them falling short? What is one way you can encourage the organization to change?
13. What specific skills are required for leaders in your organization, according to your HR department or recent job descriptions? What are ways you can develop these skills, inside and outside of work?
14. How can men be better supporters of women? What should they stop doing? And what can they do more of?
15. What are relationships like between women at your office? What are ways you've seen women support each other—and what are other ways you can do the same?

ABOUT THE CONTRIBUTORS

Amy Bernstein, *Women at Work* cohost, is the editor of *Harvard Business Review* and vice president and executive editorial director of Harvard Business Publishing. Follow her on Twitter @asbernstein2185.

Sarah Green Carmichael, *Women at Work* cohost (seasons 1–2), is an editor and columnist at Bloomberg Opinion and a former executive editor at *Harvard Business Review*. Follow her on Twitter @skgreen.

Amy Gallo, *Women at Work* cohost, is a contributing editor at *Harvard Business Review* and the author of the *HBR Guide to Dealing with Conflict* (Harvard Business Review Press, 2017) and *Getting Along: How to Work with Anyone (Even Difficult People)* (Harvard Business Review Press, 2022). She writes and speaks about workplace dynamics. Watch her TEDx talk on conflict and follow her on Twitter @amyegallo.

Nicole Torres, *Women at Work* cohost (seasons 1–4), is an editor at Bloomberg Opinion based in London and a former senior editor at *Harvard Business Review.*

Rania H. Anderson is an international keynote speaker, author, and executive business coach who transforms the way men and women work together. She is the author of *WE: Men, Women, and the Decisive Formula for Winning at Work* and *Undeterred.*

Nina A. Bowman is a managing partner at Paravis Partners, an executive coaching and leadership development firm. She is an executive coach to senior-level leaders and leadership teams, and publicly speaks on issues of strategic leadership, leadership presence, interpersonal effectiveness, and career development. She is also a contributing author to the *HBR Guide to Coaching Employees* (Harvard Business Review Press, 2014) and the *HBR Guide to Thinking Strategically* (Harvard Business Review Press, 2019).

Jodi-Ann Burey is a sought-after speaker and writer who works at the intersections of race, culture, and health equity. She is the creator and host of *Black Cancer,* a podcast about the lives of people of color told through their cancer journeys. Her TEDx talk, "The Myth of Bringing Your Full Authentic Self to Work," embodies her disruption of traditional narratives about racism at work.

Pamela Carlton is the president of Springboard, a consultancy on cross-cultural leadership, and the coauthor of the research report *Eve of Change: Women Redefining Corporate America*. She earned JD and MBA degrees at Yale and was a managing director in investment banking at JPMorgan Chase. Prior to that, she was at Morgan Stanley.

Brianna Barker Caza is an associate professor of management in the Bryan School of Business and Economics at the University of North Carolina at Greensboro.

Paola Cecchi-Dimeglio, is a behavioral economist and faculty chair of the Executive Leadership Research Initiative for Women and Minority Attorneys at Harvard Law School (CLP) and Harvard Kennedy School (WAPPP). In addition to her work in academia, she is the CEO of a niche behavioral and data science consulting firm (www.pcdconsultinggroup.com), and she develops debiasing software. Follow her on Twitter @HLSPaola.

Stephanie Creary is an assistant professor of management at the University of Pennsylvania's Wharton School.

Tasha Eurich, is an organizational psychologist, researcher, and *New York Times*–bestselling author. She is the principal of the Eurich Group, a boutique executive development firm that helps companies—from startups to the

Fortune 100—succeed by improving the effectiveness of their leaders and teams. Her newest book, *Insight,* delves into the connection between self-awareness and success in the workplace.

Kristi Hedges is a senior leadership coach who specializes in executive communications and the author of *The Inspiration Code: How the Best Leaders Energize People Every Day* and *The Power of Presence: Unlock Your Potential to Influence and Engage Others.* She's the founder of the Hedges Company and Element North Leadership Development, as well as a faculty member at Georgetown University's Institute for Transformational Leadership.

Sylvia Ann Hewlett is an economist, the CEO of Hewlett Consulting Partners, and the founder and chair emeritus of Coqual, formerly the Center for Talent Innovation. She is the author of 14 critically acclaimed books, including *Off-Ramps and On-Ramps*; *Forget a Mentor, Find a Sponsor*; *Executive Presence*; and *The Sponsor Effect.*

Ronit Kark is a professor of leadership and organization studies at Bar-Ilan University in Israel, and at the School of Business, The University of Exeter, in the United Kingdom. She founded the Gender in the Field graduate program for social activism. She is a senior editor of the *Leadership Quarterly* and has received the Scholarly Contributions to Educational

Practice Advancing Women in Leadership award from the Academy of Management. She studies leadership and its interplay with gender, creativity, and identities at work and play, and has worked as a consultant with many executives, teams, and organizations. She is an academic nomad, traveling internationally to give keynote presentations and guest lectures on leadership topics.

Rebecca Knight is a senior correspondent at *Insider*, covering careers and the workplace. Previously she was a freelance journalist and a lecturer at Wesleyan University. Her work has been published in the *New York Times*, *USA Today*, and the *Financial Times*.

Jamie J. Ladge is an associate professor at the D'Amore-McKim School of Business at Northeastern University and a distinguished research professor at the University of Exeter Business School. Her book, *Maternal Optimism: Forging Positive Paths through Work and Motherhood*, explores the uniqueness of each working mother's journey to integrate career and family.

Anne Welsh McNulty has invested in elevating entrepreneurial leaders and nurturing promising students for over 25 years as cofounder and president of the McNulty Foundation. A trailblazer for women in finance, she was a managing director of Goldman Sachs and a senior executive of the Goldman Sachs Hedge Fund Strategies Group.

Alyson Meister is a professor of leadership and organizational behavior at IMD Business School in Lausanne, Switzerland. Specializing in the development of globally oriented, adaptive, and inclusive organizations, she has worked with thousands of executives, teams, and organizations from professional services to industrial goods and technology. Her research has been widely published, and in 2021 she was recognized as a Thinkers50 Radar thought leader. Follow her on Twitter @alymeister.

Candice Morgan was formerly the Head of Inclusion & Diversity at Pinterest.

Curt Nickisch is a senior editor at *Harvard Business Review,* where he makes podcasts and cohosts *HBR IdeaCast.* He earned an MBA from Boston University and previously reported for NPR, Marketplace, WBUR, and *Fast Company.* He speaks *ausgezeichnet* German and binges history podcasts. Follow him on Twitter @CurtNickisch.

Tina Opie is the founder of Opie Consulting Group, where she advises large firms in the financial services, entertainment, media, beauty, educational, and healthcare industries. She is an award-winning researcher, consultant, associate professor of management at Babson College, and visiting scholar at Harvard Business School. Her work has appeared in such outlets as *O Magazine,* the *Washington Post*, the *Boston Globe*, and *Harvard Business Review*. She is also a regular commentator on HBR's *Women at Work* podcast and Greater Boston's NPR affiliate television station WGBH.

Cindy Pace, is Vice President, Global Chief Diversity, Equity and Inclusion Officer at MetLife and lecturer of organizational leadership at Columbia University. She has over 20 years of corporate management and leadership experience working in financial services, healthcare, and biopharmaceuticals. Her business insights and research has been featured in the *Financial Times*, *Fortune*, *Forbes*, *Harvard Business Review*, TED +Brightline, and the book *Women's Leadership Journeys: Stories, Research, and Novel Perspectives*.

Shannon Huffman Polson is one of the first women to fly the Apache helicopter in the United States Army. In addition to her military service, she earned an MBA at the Tuck School of Business at Dartmouth and spent five years leading and managing in the corporate sector at Guidant and Microsoft. She is the founder of the Grit Institute, the author of *The Grit Factor: Courage, Resilience, and Leadership in the Most Male-Dominated Organization in the World* and the memoir *North of Hope: A Daughter's Arctic Journey*, and speaks frequently on topics related to leadership, courage, resilience, and grit.

Lakshmi Ramarajan is an associate professor at Harvard Business School.

Erin Reid is an associate professor at McMaster University's DeGroote School of Business.

Rebecca Shambaugh is an internationally recognized leadership expert, author, and keynote speaker. She's the president of SHAMBAUGH, a global leadership development organization, and the founder of Women in Leadership and Learning (WILL).

Alexis Nicole Smith is an assistant professor of management at Oklahoma State University. She earned her PhD in management at Tulane University and her BA from Rice University. Her research interests include gender dynamics, social identity, bias, and workplace diversity.

David G. Smith is an associate professor in the Johns Hopkins Carey Business School. He is a coauthor, with W. Brad Johnson, of *Good Guys: How Men Can Be Better Allies for Women in the Workplace* and *Athena Rising: How and Why Men Should Mentor Women.*

Amy Jen Su is cofounder and managing partner of Paravis Partners, a premier executive coaching and leadership development firm. For the past two decades, she has coached CEOs, executives, and rising stars in organizations. She is the author of *The Leader You Want to Be: Five Essential Principles for Bringing Out Your Best Self—Every Day* (Harvard Business Review Press, 2019), and a coauthor, with Muriel Maignan Wilkins, of *Own the Room: Discover Your Signature Voice to Master Your Leadership Presence* (Harvard Business Review Press, 2013).

Ruchika Tulshyan is the founder of Candour, an inclusion strategy firm. She writes regularly for the *New York Times* and *Harvard Business Review* on workplace inclusion. Her latest book is *Inclusion on Purpose: An Intersectional Approach to Creating a Culture of Belonging at Work*.

Marla Baskerville Watkins is an associate professor in the Management and Organizational Department at Northeastern University. She earned her PhD in organizational behavior at Tulane University, MEd from the University of Georgia, and BS from Howard University. Her research interests include power and influence, gender and diversity, and expressions of sexuality at work.

Muriel Maignan Wilkins is a cofounder and managing partner of Paravis Partners, a boutique executive coaching and leadership development firm. She is an adviser and coach to C-suite executives and has a nearly 20-year track record of helping leaders take their effectiveness to the next level. She is a coauthor, with Amy Jen Su, of *Own* *the Room: Discover Your Signature Voice to Master Your Leadership Presence* (Harvard Business Review Press, 2013) and host of the HBR Presents podcast *Coaching Real Leaders.*

Wei Zheng is an associate professor of management and the Richard R. Roscitt Chair in Leadership at Stevens Institute of Technology. Her research centers on inclusive leadership and addresses practical questions such as what inclusive leadership looks like, which organizational practices enhance diversity, how individuals grow into leaders, and what help women leaders need to navigate gendered organizations. She has studied leadership in corporate, entrepreneurial, national laboratory, and faith-based organizations, and has conducted in-depth interviews with more than 120 top-level executives in the United States. Her research work has appeared in outlets such as the *Leadership Quarterly*, *Journal of Management*, and *Human Relations*. She is leading the School of Business' effort on gathering and disseminating leadership knowledge from exemplars to all leadership learners through Stevens Leadership Portal. She regularly speaks at and consults with organizations on leadership and diversity.

Women *at* Work

Inspiring conversations, advancing together

ABOUT THE PODCAST

Women face gender discrimination throughout our careers. It doesn't have to derail our ambitions, but how do we prepare to deal with it? There's no workplace orientation session about narrowing the wage gap, standing up to interrupting male colleagues, or taking on many other issues we encounter at work. So HBR staffers Amy Bernstein, Amy Gallo, and Emily Caulfield are untangling some of the knottiest problems. They interview experts on gender, tell stories about their own experiences, and give lots of practical advice to help you succeed in spite of the obstacles.

Listen and subscribe:

Apple Podcasts, Google Podcasts, Spotify, RSS